# POWER STRENGTH & PERSERVERANCE

*What women know about other women, but search for in themselves.*

By

PATRICIA M. ANNINO

ISBN # 978-1-7359630-0-6 (print)

ISBN # 978-1-7359630-1-3 (eBook)

*To Nan-b de Gaspé Beaubien, a woman of elegance and power.*

# Table of Contents

# PREFACE

**"Believe me, judicious mother, do not make of your daughter a decent man as if to give lie to nature. Make a decent woman of her and you will be sure she will be worth more for herself and for us."**

*-Jean-Jaques Rosseau*

Five years ago, I was stuck. At a gut level knew I was going to a knife fight with a butter knife. A critical meeting loomed with a man who held all the financial cards. I knew I had to change the deal I had with him. A preliminary conversation had not gone well. He told me why he would not change his mind. I had the presence of mind to ask for another meeting a week later and he agreed to that.

In advance of that meeting, marshalling my skills as a lawyer, I sat down and wrote out all the reasons the deal should change in my favor. (I had added value, revenue had increased x amount etc.). I stared at the paper and I knew in my heart this strategy was not going to work. Bill could anticipate all that was on this list and he had already sent me a subtle indication he was entrenched in his position. "He who holds the gold rules." My meeting was lip service. He would hear me out and not change the deal. He knew that, and I knew that.

I needed a different perspective. I met with an organizational psychologist who asked me to begin the negotiation, pretending she was the guy. A lawyer by training, I laid out my case.

She listened, and then explained to me that my presentation was exactly what Bill was expecting. He would negotiate with me, lawyer to lawyer, and win.

She then asked me who I thought was the most powerful woman in the world. I answered, "Hillary Clinton."

She did not agree. "The most powerful woman in the world is Queen Elizabeth, and the two most powerful words she uses are 'Thank you.'"

She asked me to pause, reset my mind and begin with a softer approach.

I took her advice. I started the meeting thanking him for taking the time to meet with me and thinking about the discussion. I mentioned a few points he had made along the way and told him I understood that his point of view had merit. I knew, because of the value I brought to the table, that he thought my ideas did too. He sat back and looked at me.

In that instance I felt a shift.

He had anticipated an aggressive stance and was ready to pounce to defend his position. Instead, he dropped the offense and listened. Changing the tone was critical. Changing the tone changed the conversation and changed the power. It disarmed him. We had a productive discussion and reached a deal.

I realized that my approach had placated the male ego. Bill had the power going into the conversation. By not threatening that power by aggressively pushing my points, I had gotten him to listen and to reason.

I flashed back to an incident that had happened to me while working as a partner in a small law firm in my late 20s. My "boss" (a man 30 years my senior) laid out his plan to take my guaranteed salary away and put me on commission, telling me I had the ability to bring in significant revenue and a commission structure would incentivize me. Reading from a legal pad and showing me numbers, he explained this was in my favor and I would make a lot more money.

I panicked. I had rent to pay, bills to pay and a lifestyle to maintain. I had never heard of a lawyer on commission. I did not negotiate. Instead I went home and resigned. He was flabbergasted and held my decision to quit against me.

It took me years to understand that something else was going on - probably a cash shortage or revenue drop - and finding my voice could have mattered. It could have opened a conversation about the firm's revenue, cash flow, that my contributions were vital and would be acknowledged financially and we needed to strike a new deal.

I thought back further to an incident that happened when I was a young associate in a mid-sized law firm. The senior partner applauded my work ethic and my ability to work well with clients. He kept assigning more and more work to me and I kept doing more and more work. Summer came and I rushed out to buy new underwear.

I'd had no time in my personal life for anything - even laundry. I was going for the "A", the "atta girl", the "star." It never occurred to me to go back to him and negotiate. It never occurred to me to say, "Whoa, I am doing the work of four people and this is not sustainable." Another law firm approached me and even though I was learning a great deal where I was, I gave my notice and jumped. The senior partner was flabbergasted and told me I was making a mistake. He said that with my work ethic and talent I would have had a brilliant future there.

Why did I not negotiate before jumping? Why did I think the power and value was one-sided? Although I was young I do not think that was the reason. It was, quite frankly, because the thought never occurred to me.

I realize today that those anecdotes underscore the lack of confidence young women tend to have in the work place - the mindset that their abilities are fixed (hence the certainty that working on commission would mean lost revenue) and that they have to strive for the gold star and be perfect, rather than think more self-confidently in terms of growth and moving ahead.

Why did it take me so long, so many decades, to recognize my power as a woman?

Thinking about these incidents started an internal dialogue. What is feminine power? What does it mean to be a woman in a post-feminist, #MeToo generation world? Feminine power is not new, yet how does one think about it or learn about it? Certainly, no one in school ever taught me anything about it.

How do you know what your power is? What is the source of your power? What is your relationship with your power? How does a woman keep her power, protect her power, use her power? Is her power strategic? How does feminine power differ from masculine power? Is someone undercutting your power? Who? How do you keep it when others try to take it away? When should you use your power and why? Why is it only discussed with careers and work? What is feminine power at home? In the community? In society?

These are the questions that prompted this book.

# Chapter 1:

# Feminism Power Struggles

**"I do not wish women to have power over men; but over themselves."**
*-Mary Shelley (author of Frankenstein)*

Today it is hard to think about female power without addressing feminism. The word, "feminism" conjures up passion for some, power for some, anger for others, and wincing from some young women. Its connotation in popular culture is just as varied as those reactions.

To me, feminism today is the individual ability of each woman to compose her own life, navigate the hurdles and obstacles which will inevitably come her way, claim her power, and understand herself and her role individually and collectively in family, and society.

Feminism is complicated. To understand more about it I began to think about why it began and what it means. I believe the feminist movement is not just a struggle by women to gain power in a "man's world." Feminism is a continuous power struggle among women in search of their individual lives and their collective role in society.

The evolution of the feminist movement has been shaped by powerful women agreeing and disagreeing with other powerful women. As Gloria Steinem said. "You can't tell the story of the women's movement through the story of one person; we have to tell this story in the collective."[1]

The disagreements voiced by the many smart, intelligent and, thoughtful women are as important shapers of where we are today as the agreements of those who propelled the movement forward. The connections and the collisions all weave together to where we are today and raise interesting questions about what the future holds for women - individually and collectively.

Feminism (in its first wave) began when Elizabeth Cady Stanton and Lucretia Mott were whisked off to a roped-off women's area (out of the sight of men) at the 1840 World Anti-Slavery Convention. Their anger and frustration led to the planning for the two-day Seneca Falls Convention of 1848, the first women's rights convention in the United States. It launched the women's suffrage movement. Two hundred women met in a church in upstate New York to discuss the "social, civil, and religious condition and rights of women."[2]

Elizabeth Cady Stanton organized the convention and delivered her "Declaration of Sentiments and Resolutions" speech.[3] Modeled on the Declaration of Independence, the premise of the speech was that "the history of mankind is a history of repeated injuries and usurpations on the part of men toward women, having in direct object, the establishment of an absolute tyranny over her" and included a list of 16 "grievances." The Declaration of Sentiments and Resolutions hailed groundbreaking demands, such as holding men to the same moral standards as women and stating that anti-women laws had no authority.[4]

The "grievances" included the lack of woman's suffrage, participation and representation in government, woman's lack of property rights in marriage, inequality in divorce laws, and inequality in education and employment opportunities. It resolved that "women being invested by the Creator with the same capabilities and the same consciousness of responsibility for their exercise, it is demonstrably the right and duty of women, equally with men, to promote every righteous cause by every righteous means; and especially in regard to the great subjects of morals and religion, it is self- evidently her right to participate with her brother in teaching them, both in private and public, by writing, and by speaking, by any instrumentalities proper to be used and in any assemblies proper to be heard."[5]

The Declaration was signed by 68 women and 32 men, many of whom were husbands or family members of the women present. It is interesting to note that the vote for the Declaration did not unanimously support the woman's right to vote because of concerns at the time that it was too controversial and would adversely impact other rights the women were fighting for.

In 1920 (more than 70 years after the Seneca Falls Convention with only one signer of the Declaration of Sentiments still living) Congress passed the 19th Amendment granting women the right to vote. This was the most significant legislative accomplishment of the first wave of feminism.

Their thoughts and stance had a respected opponent. There was a very powerful female counter movement - the anti-suffragists. Professor Catherine Cole Mabretti, in "The Burden of the Ballot: The Woman's Anti-Suffrage Movement," presents the ideas of an almost forgotten group of women who believed that woman's true power lay in obedience, not political expression. "Families held the nation together, and mothers held families together. In motherhood resided the essence of femininity and feminine power, for here women acquired indirect but real political influence through husbands, male relatives and especially future voters, their sons."[6] Note the word "indirect."

The author of *Rebecca of Sunnybrook Farm*, Kate Wiggin, explained that, women should "be a helpful, stimulating, inspiring force in the world rather than a useful and influential factor in politics."[7]

On the question of whether mothers could be expected to tend to their responsibilities from a voting booth, writer Caroline Corbin warned, "When political rewards are offered to women, do you not believe that many - and those not of the weak and ignorant, but of the more gifted and intellectual - will be tempted to forgo marriage and motherhood for the sake of winning them? Woe betide the land which thus offers its political trusts as premiums for childless women! Even women who might still consent to bear children might be inclined, as some suffragists proposed, to leave their children's care to institutions, or to husbands who might be asked to share in child-care duties."[8]

The anti-suffragettes believed that by foregoing their traditional roles, women would disrupt the family - the basis of social structure. While their ideas were controversial, these women found obedience more empowering than equality with men.

The first wave of feminism was much more than a battle for rights. It was also a struggle by intelligent women against intelligent women to sort out what it meant to be a woman. It was about searching for what being female meant independently and collectively.

That question travels through time and is still here today.

The second wave of feminism began a century after the Seneca Falls Convention, with thinkers such as Simone de Beauvoir whose book, *The Second Sex*,[9] was released in France in 1949 and the United States in 1953. Simone De Beauvoir and Marybeth Timmermann, in the essay, "Femininity: The Trap" reject femininity.[10] De Beauvoir writes, "I myself think there is no myth more irritating and more false than that of the eternal feminine which was invented, with the help of women, by men, who describe her as intuitive, charming, sensitive. These powerful feminine qualities are weaknesses. Women must be 'taken in' by men's flattery to believe that these feminine qualities are valuable."

She dismissed the feminine roles of wife and mother as unimportant and regressive. "In the past women were housewives and mothers and as such no principles of progress could come from them. As guardians of the home they were turned toward tradition, toward the dead past. Men alone invented the future." She totally disregarded the inspirational power of women or that women directly shaped the future by raising children. She claimed that a woman must be masculine to succeed professionally. "A woman who does not work outside the home cannot have a fully developed personality."

Feminism's second wave exploded in 1963 with Betty Friedan's book, *The Feminine Mystique*.[11] This book was considered a phenomenon and sold three million copies in three years. It rallied against "the problem that has no name" – the systemic sexism that taught women that their place was in their home. Freidan posited that women were right to be unhappy - they were being ripped off in a world that refused to allow them to exercise their creative and intellectual faculties. What is interesting about Friedan's book is that many of the ideas she posits were already in the culture. Her book and its exceptional reach into the hands of so many women in the white middle class culture gave these women permission to be angry.

Yet, not only was Friedan's book challenged by women who did not work, it was also challenged by women who did. Betty Friedan and Gloria Steinem clashed in their views of the movement. Gloria Steinem commented that Freidan's book did a lot for women who were married and in the suburbs and had an education they were not using and wanted to use, who thought that they had a right to a profession. Steinem's problem with Friedan's message was that it was reformist, not feminist. It was not talking about all women, including Steinem herself who was single and working in New York City and did not understand how the message related to her.[12]

Friedan warned that the movement would be irreparably damaged if it did not purge itself of "female chauvinism" and begin to work with men instead of against them. In an article in *McCall's Magazine* Friedan wrote, "The assumption that women have any moral or spiritual superiority as a class or that men share some brute insensitivity as a class - this is male chauvinism in reverse; it is female sexism. It is, in fact, female chauvinism and those who preach or practice it seem to me to be corrupting our movement for equality and inviting a backlash that endangers the very real gains we have won these past years."[13]

Friedan specifically criticized Steinem and Bella Abzug. She accused Miss Steinem of dismissing marriage as prostitution and assuming that "no woman would ever want to go to bed with a man if she didn't need to sell her body for bread or a mink coat."

Steinem rebutted Friedan saying, "Having been falsely accused by the male establishment journalists of liking men too much, I am now being falsely accused by a woman establishment journalist of not liking them enough."

Bella Abzug rebutted Friedan by saying "Once again Betty Friedan has exercised her right to be wrong. I've never asked anyone to vote for me only because I am a woman."

Other women opposed Friedan's line of thinking - and more generally the feminist movement. Perhaps the most effective and well known was Phyllis Schlafly whose message was quite different and based on her belief that "the family assures a woman the most precious and important right of all - the right to keep her own baby and to be supported and protected in the enjoyment of watching her baby grow and develop." The movement Schlafly led competed successfully with the feminists on the left with a different philosophy. Her grassroots movement and her best-selling book, *A Choice Not an Echo* was an important part of the conservative movement. She set out to defeat the Equal Rights Amendment and succeeded.[14]

When Betty Friedan attacked her in a debate and shouted, "I'd like to burn you at the stake!" Schlafly replied, "I'm glad you said that because it just shows the intemperate nature of proponents of the ERA." Reflecting, Phyllis Schlafly said, "The feminist movement taught women to see themselves as victims of an oppressive patriarchy in which their true worth will never be recognized and any success is beyond their reach. Self-imposed victimhood is not a recipe for happiness."

Conflict among women about feminism and power was as prevalent as the conflict about men and culture. Tactics were employed. When asked if Steinem would debate Schlafly, her answer was no. "We agreed that only women who were not well known would debate her because if I debated her, it would only increase her argument and fan her movement."[15]

When asked more recently what she thought about Sarah Palin and Michelle Bachmann who may never have achieved power without Gloria and her gang, she answered, "You know what you're saying is important when the power structure brings in people who look like you and think like them."

All of this is complicated, and so is Gloria Steinem, her views on femininity, and what the relationship between femininity and feminism is. In 1986 she teamed with photographer George Barris and wrote the text for the glossy, coffee-table book, *Marilyn: Norma Jean*. Why would Gloria Steinem, one of the most influential women in the feminist movement select the classic, femme fatale, Marilyn Monroe as a person to write a book about?

When asked, Steinem said, "Marilyn was an exaggerated illustration of so many things of what's wrong with Freud, of how devastating it is to tell women they're not real women unless they have children - one of her great tragedies is that she could not have children - and of identifying value in terms of how we look, instead of what is in our hearts and our heads, of encouraging women to remain children. The penalty of encouraging men to think that women are nonjudgmental and passive and children, is that they (men) come to expect a sexual relationship without any of the challenge of an *adult* female."[16]

To me, externally Marilyn is the epitome of feminine. She is beautiful and seductive, brainy (although pretending not to be), yet charming. She loved men and she seemed to enjoy the "dance." Because of her femininity and her beauty (and of course her talent), Marilyn was successful in her career in a business world that was at the time controlled by men.

As I read Steinem's text on Marilyn and her interviews about Marilyn it struck me that Steinem hit on a fundamental part of the struggle of feminism - the internal struggle thinking women have today about who they are inside and who they are outside and how hard it can be to reconcile the two forces. Perhaps the reason for Steinem writing the text in the Monroe book was not to show the multi dimensions of Marilyn but to look at a contemporary peer of equal beauty and similar childhood upheaval and search inside herself for what it meant to be beautiful and brainy. This inherent clash between feminine and feminism was at its strongest during the second wave.

The power of the second wave resulted in The Equal Pay Act of 1963, Title IX and in 1973 Supreme Court decision legalizing abortion, Roe v. Wade.

Feminism's third wave began sometime around 1991, when the Anita Hill case jumpstarted an avalanche of sexual harassment complaints and fights against workplace sexual harassment. The third wave movement was more diffuse. At a 2002 conference at Barnard College the third wave feminists expressed concern about the second wave feminists. They believed that while feminists in the second wave were focused on fighting for gender equality in the workplace, abortion rights and economic parity, those in the third wave were looking at a wider range of topics through the feminist lens, everything from arts to prison reform.[17]

Feminism's fourth wave began around 2006 and drives the #MeToo and Times Up Movements, with the goal of holding powerful men accountable for their behavior toward women.

With all that women have accomplished, is feminism relevant now?

Joanna Williams (raised a feminist and no longer a feminist), in her book, *Women v. Feminism,*[18] exposes today's victim feminism and tells the story of how a once valiant movement for equality and freedom has devolved into a male bashing grievance fest. She posits that there has never been a better time to be a woman. Thanks to those feminists who fought for liberation, young women today have freedom and opportunities their grandmothers could barely have imagined. Girls do better at school than boys and are more likely to go to university. Women are taking more of the top jobs and the gender pay gap is just about gone. Yet, rather than encouraging women to seize the new possibilities before them, contemporary feminism tells them they are still oppressed. In fact, she argues, feminism today must continually find new controversies to keep itself relevant.

Williams thinks we have historical amnesia as to what life was like before the sexual revolution, before sexual liberation for women. She writes, "We run a real risk in actually trivializing some of the far more serious offenses if we speak about knee touching, clumsy flirtations, unwanted kisses, in the same breath as rape and sexual assault." Williams stresses that today's feminism is obsessed with trivial issues - skinny models, badly phrased jokes and misplaced compliments and focuses on the regulation of male behavior, not female empowerment, pitching men and women against each other in a never ending gender war that benefits no one. She concludes that feminism today does women no favors and it is time we were all liberated from the gender wars.

So where are we? Perhaps we should look back at the beginning of the founding of the country with deep respect for the personal power of Abigail Adams, the wife of a president and the mother of a president. She worked the farm, managed the household affairs and family economic affairs without going into debt during the almost ten years of the American Revolution when she and her husband were separated. She faced many challenges and had confidence in her own power in changing turbulent times.

During the war she ran the family farm for four years and during that time she had significant issues due to her lack of experience with active management, inflation and with procuring labor. But she succeeded. "I hardly know how I have got through these things," she wrote her husband, "but it gives me great pleasure to say that they are done because I know it will be an Ease to your mind."

In return John praised her. "I begin to be jealous, that our Neighbors will think Affairs more discreetly conducted in my Absence than at any other time."... "Gen. Warren writes me, that my Farm never looked better, than when he last saw it, and that Mrs.- was like to outshine all the Farmers."

Abigail knew that land was wealth and during her separation from her husband she negotiated and acquired land. This is particularly profound because women could not own land. She was negotiating on her own for land that would be in her husband's name. And that was fine with her.

In addition to her business interests and supporting her family she read a great deal (Moliere, Milton, Rosseau, Shakespeare, Pope, Addison, history books, travel books, poetry, and literature on the war and its repercussions).

She had her own opinions. She strongly believed in education and she strove to improve her intellect. In a letter to her husband she wrote that she hoped "that our new Constitution may be distinguished for learning and virtue. If we mean to have Heroes, Statesman and Philosophers we should have learned women." Her husband concurred in a letter back to her, "Your Sentiments on the Importance of Education in Women, are exactly agreeable to my own."

Despite the cultural stigma against women in politics in her time, Abigail was open in her discussions on politics with her husband. In a letter to him she confessed, "my pen is always freer than my tongue."

Abigail and John Adams had a strong marriage that lasted 54 years. Historian Edith Gelles[19] (who spent 30 years researching Abigail Adams) notes that "each of them was generous towards the other. Each one was giving towards the other and sacrificed for each other and respected each other." Gelles notes of their relationship, "Abigail, who didn't really want to go on serving the public after John's vice-presidency, did so because she never questioned John's public service. She was loyal to him. She became his closest confidant and probably, advisor... Abigail was his best ally, and because she was intelligent, well-informed, and totally sympathetic with him, she was devoted to his politics. She was probably the best-informed and most reliable advisor to a president until Eleanor Roosevelt in the 20th century."

Gelles also writes, however, that Abigail disapproved of women who breached her code of domestic behavior. Much as she was compelled in the absence of her husband to take on unfeminine roles, she believed it was extraordinary, aberrant, expedient, and unnatural. She often referred to her conduct as a patriotic sacrifice for her country. Gelles notes that Abigail believed women were domestic beings, that their primary functions were within the home as wife and mother. She believed that women, the weaker sex, were meant to be submissive, dependent upon and protected by men. She also believed that women were as intelligent as men although the intelligence was to be applied differently by men and women. She liked women, saw dignity in the domestic function, and had no aspiration for changing their traditional role.

In a 1776 letter to her husband Abigail wrote, "by the way in the new Code of Laws which I suppose it will be necessary for you to make, I desire you would Remember the Ladies, and be more generous and favorable the them than your ancestors." ... "Do not put such unlimited power into the hands of the Husbands. Remember all men would be tyrants if they could."[20]

She was a woman who faced many personal obstacles, challenges, and opportunities in turbulent times. She took responsibility for her life and her actions. She did what she needed to do when life threw her off balance. She made her life work, protected her family (financially and morally), maintained a strong marriage, maintained strong friendships, participated in social reform, and was an active participant in the founding of America. Through it all Abigail Adams kept inner integrity. No matter what she faced, the touchstones of her own power remained resolute.

Some commentators have said that Abigail Adams was a feminist; others have said that she was not. I posit today that any label of "feminist" does not matter today. There are no barriers for a woman to accomplish what she wants personally or professionally. What mattered to Abigail Adams and what matters now is knowing oneself, understanding what one wants and having the personal power to accomplish it. Abigail Adams did that.

The tapestry of the legacies of these women make it clear that it is up to each of us individually to step into our own power and lead the life we wish to live, value ourselves and our contributions in order accomplish great things in the world, and, in doing so, protect ourselves, those we love and the organizations we care about.

# Chapter 2:

# Marriage and Power

**"Marriage is not a noun: it's a verb. It isn't something you get. It's something you do. It's the way you love your partner every day."**

*-Barbara De Angelis*

Gloria Steinem, who was famously quoted back in the 1970s and 80s saying, "A woman without a man is like a fish without a bicycle," "Marriage is slavery," and "A woman's total instinct for gambling is satisfied by marriage," ended up marrying for the first time at age 66 to David Bale, who died of lymphoma three years later. She was his primary caregiver during the last year of his life.

Four years after his death, she was asked by a reporter why she changed her mind about marriage. She answered, "I didn't change; marriage changed. We spent thirty years in the United States changing the marriage laws. If I had married when I was supposed to get married, I would have lost my name, my legal residence, my credit rating, and many of my civil rights. That's not true anymore. It's possible to make an equal marriage."[21]

She also said, when discussing her marriage, that she was "happy, surprised and… hopes that this proves that feminism is about the ability to choose what is right at each time of our lives."

Abigail Adams married John Adams in very different times, but theirs was a marriage of equals in some respects. Abigail's intelligence, wit, wisdom, and strength flourished alongside that of her husband, lending legitimacy to the claim of a woman's equal status. But it was not an equal marriage. Under the laws at the time Abigail had very little control over the kind of work she performed, over her reproductive life or probably over her sex life.[22]

Marriage with its obligations became her destiny and that world presupposed a very clear separation of male and female spheres that certainly were not equal but hierarchically organized. The lens through which Abigail viewed her world revealed a patriarchy in which it was her destiny to live in the domestic sphere under the terms that John Adams's work and choices about place, marriage, and style governed.

Abigail accepted that world and was by all accounts successful in it. In their marriage there was a presumption of psychological equality between John and Abigail that Abigail expected, and John found intoxicating.[23] She married a man who loved the fact, as he put it, that she was "saucy" and a woman who was simultaneously capable of unconditional love and personal independence.[24]

Phyllis Schlafly's husband, Fred, loved and respected her success and frequently quipped, "I regret that I have one wife to give to my country."[25] In her wedding vows, Phyllis promised to cherish Fred, but omitted the word "obey." Phyllis called their marriage (which produced six children and endured to Fred's death) an "intellectual partnership."

In a 1978 *Good Morning America* interview Fred was asked if Phyllis wore the pants in the family. He laughed and said, "No, she doesn't. She is very submissive."[26]

Phyllis agreed and said Fred was the boss in the family. Phyllis traveled with young children and a baby nurse who cared for the children while on the speaking circuit, called herself a more traditional wife and would often start her speeches, "I want to thank my husband, Fred, for letting me come here." She wrote that 1964 was the most productive year of her life. "I was running the Illinois Federation of Republican Women. I wrote a *Choice Not an Echo*, and I self-published it. I went to the Republican Convention, wrote a second book, *The Gravediggers*, gave speeches for Barry Goldwater and had a baby."[27]

With all these accomplishments Phyllis always chose to characterize herself as "a housewife."[28]

Amelia Earhart, who was married to George P. Putnam (of the publishing dynasty) until her death, wrote a letter in 1923 to Putnam in which she tried to extract a promise of equal partnership and ensure that he, and marriage, would not keep her from pursuing her dreams. "Let us not interfere with the other's work or play. I cannot agree to endure at all times the confinement of even an attractive cage."[29]

As the couple left their no-frills wedding ceremony, the judge addressed Earhart as "Mrs. Putnam," to which she responded, "Please, Sir, I prefer Miss Earhart." Amelia did not use the word "obey" in her wedding vows and referred to her marriage as a "partnership" with "dual controls."

Perhaps each of these very different marriages endured because in each case the woman knew what she wanted, was able to articulate it, considered marriage to be a partnership, thought through her choice of husband, and did what was needed to make it work. Each of these women achieved significant personal and professional accomplishments, were role models and impacted society.

A strongly supportive husband propelling his wife forward is powerful too. The late Ruth Bader Ginsburg emphasized that her husband, Marty, "was the only young man I dated who cared I had a brain." Ginsburg is admired for her legal achievements, especially toward ensuring gender equality and her 56-year marriage put that theory into practice. Ginsburg and her husband both worked outside the home decades before that was the norm. They split child-care and domestic duties. She relocated for his career and he relocated for her career.[30]

"I betray no secret in reporting that, without him, I would not have gained a seat on the Supreme Court," Ginsberg wrote in the New York Times. She quoted Ron Klain, the associate White House counsel at the time of the nomination, who said, "I would say definitely and for the record, though Ruth Bader Ginsburg should have been picked for the Supreme Court anyway, she would not have been picked for the Supreme Court if her husband had not done everything possible to make it happen."[31] In her Supreme Court nomination hearing Ginsburg stated, "I have had the good fortune to share life with a partner truly extraordinary for this generation, a man who believed at age 18 when we met, and believes today, that a woman's work, whether at home or on the job, is as important as a man's."[32]

In 2010 Ginsburg found a note he had left for her.

*"6/17/10*

*My dearest Ruth-*

*You are the only person I have loved in my life, setting aside a bit, parents and kids and their kids, and I have admired and loved you almost since the day we first met at Cornell some 56 years ago.*

*What a treat it has been to watch you progress to the very top of the legal world!!*

*I will be in JH Medical Center until Friday, June 25, I believe and between then and now I shall think hard on my remaining health and life, and whether on balance the time has come for me to tough it out or take leave of life because the loss of quality now simply overwhelms. I hope you will support where I come out, but I understand you may not. I will not love you a jot less."*

*Marty"*[33]

Martin Ginsburg died at home shortly after that.

Power in a marriage is not always apparent to those who observe the marriage. Political marriages can show power to the outside world which is different than the power of the woman within the marriage. The indirect power of some First Ladies has been significant. In the marriage of Barbara and George H.W. Bush, Barbara's exigent manner is balanced by a universal graciousness. One role Barbara Bush took on was to judge each man and woman by the standard of his or her devotion to George Bush. Yet no one around them doubted that she had great power to influence her husband. Some went so far as to suggest that she was his number-one political advisor.[34]

Michelle Obama, a powerful woman in her own right, expressed a slightly different view on her husband before he took office. "In any case the American electorate won't be treated to any displays of the adoring spouse pose perfected by Nancy Reagan, who never tweaked her husband in public and whose worshipful mask never slipped, no matter no matter how many times she sat through the same speech. I can't do that. That's not me. I love my husband. I think he's one of the most brilliant men I've ever met, and he knows that. But he's not perfect, and I don't want the world to think him to be perfect. If you look for that, then people can't try hard stuff because you might mess up. We want leaders to be bold and to try some things that may not work, because they might work and be great. I think that's one of our failings as a nation; we're looking for our leaders to be something that's not realistic, and then we're deeply disappointed when they don't live up to those unrealistic standards. So, let's shake that up a little bit. We're moving into the 21st century and life is different. We've struggled; we've grown. Let's not be hypocrites about it either. Let's not say we want one thing and then demand you be something you're not."[35]

Which spouse has the most power in a marriage? A tricky question and it turns out that at least one research study showed that in society men may have earned more income, but women have the power at home. A 2002 Iowa State University study of 72 married couples (all of whom were relatively happy and none of whom were in counseling), found that wives, on average, exhibited greater situational power in the form of domineering and dominant behaviors than their husbands during problem solving discussions, regardless of who brought up the topic.[36]

One of the researchers noted, "Women are responsible for overseeing the relationship—making sure the relationship runs, that everything gets done, and that everybody is happy." In the study each spouse was asked independently to identify a problem in his or her relationship. Most couples talked about financial or household problems. The couples were then brought together to discuss the two issues. Their conversations were videotaped, and the communication patterns coded. The researchers were looking at which spouse was more domineering (when one spouse tries to "one-up" the other spouse). They found wives were more domineering and the husbands often gave into the wives' requests, usually responding, "That sounds OK to me, honey." (Based on my personal experience one also wonders if sometimes the man capitulates because it is not an issue he feels is worth going to the mat over.)

There are many ways to think about whether a marriage works and what factors into a successful, healthy marriage. The choices we make along the way have an impact on marital success.

In today's world in many marriages both spouses work. And one may think that the one who has the gold rules, that who has and earns the money always impacts the balance of power. Harvard sociologist Alexandra Achen Killewald found that the things that increase the probability of divorce, as they relate to work at least, have changed over the past couple of decades.[37] She found that the amount of money either the husband or wife makes is not determinative; for contemporary couples, the biggest determinant is whether the husband is working full-time. She tracked 6,309 married couples between 1968 and 2013, 1684 of whom divorced or permanently separated during that time. She drew a line to account for the "quiet revolution," or the time when women could count on pursuing full-fledged careers, between the couples married before and after 1975.

In the later cohort the wife's paid or unpaid labor had little effect on her chance of divorce but the husband's breadwinning mattered. If he was employed full time, there was a 2.5 chance of splitting the next year and if he wasn't, there was a 3.3 percent chance. Her results contradicted leading explanations for why people divorce and why so many people broke up in the 70s and 80s.

She concluded that, for contemporary couples, wives can combine paid and unpaid labor in various ways without threatening the stability of their marriages. But the risk of divorce increases substantially when the husband isn't employed full-time. *While the homemaker ideal has waned in importance, the notion of the breadwinner is still hanging on.*

As a contemporary example which may illustrate the need to feel provided for, Giselle Bundchen, a supermodel has said she earns millions of dollars a year but does not spend any of it on her household. Instead her husband, Tom Brady, pays for everything because she wants to feel taken care of.[38]

One wonders if it is difficult today for women who feel that way to admit it, and for women who would prefer not to work but rather to be taken care of financially and stay at home to easily admit that too.

I remember speaking to a group of women in Chicago about 10 years ago on the topic of women and money. My target was the baby boomer woman. The gist of the presentation was that women are double inheritors; they inherit once from the parents and again from their husbands. Women need to understand money; they need to know what they have, and they need to know what happens if their spouses die. For many women, the keys to the kingdom of understanding are on the table and they walk by that table, not picking them up until disaster strikes and they are forced to do so. And then, it is to too late. So the time to think about it and understand it is now, before the crisis.

I make presentations about 40-50 times a year throughout the country on this topic and have written other books on it, so I was surprised that day when for the first time I was heckled. A young woman went to the microphone and told me I had no idea what I was talking about. She and her friends were very much aware of money, and the reality was that most of them out earned their boyfriends/husbands.

In that instant I understood the world had changed. The women in that generation (now in their 30's and 40s), when they work, are as or more successful financially than their husbands are and proud of it.

What that woman did not articulate is that although that may be true, there are other repercussions. A New York Magazine article, *Alpha Women, Beta Men,*[39] notes that for some women admitting that they are the sole financial support of the family with a stay-at-home husband is like realizing you are married to someone who drinks too much (and that should not be spoken about). The article notes that there is little evidence to show that as women acquire financial muscle, relations between the sexes have evolved successfully to accommodate a new balance of power. Neither the newly liberated alpha women nor the shell-shocked beta spouses seem comfortable with the role reversal. For women, the shift in economic power gives them new choices, not the least among them to reappraise their partners. And husbands, for their part, may find to their chagrin that being financially dependent isn't exactly a turn-on.

A pattern may evolve. First the wife starts to lose respect for her husband, then he begins to feel emasculated, and then sex dwindles to a full stop. In many cases the role reversal is the work of market forces as much as the work of personality. The husband's career is expected to take precedence, and initially it does, but then it is overtaken by the wife's career. Neither of them saw it coming, nor do they welcome it. The husband's earning power may have been a given part of the bargain.

Are those feelings mitigated if chores are shared? Many of the women I know who work full time feel the additional burden of doing all that is expected traditionally of a woman at home – the dishes, cooking, the laundry, etc. Professors Alison Byrne and Julian Barling, in their Harvard Business Review article, "*Does a Woman's High-Status Career Hurt Her Marriage? Not if her Husband Does the Laundry*,"[40] note that having higher earning power than her husband can make marriage more difficult for a wife.

For their study they developed a nine-item scale to assess wives' feelings about their status relevant to their husbands and then surveyed 209 women from executive leadership positions who held high-status roles and were in heterosexual married or common-law relationships. They also obtained data from 53 husbands.

The study's results showed that "societal norms still suggest that in heterosexual marriages, husbands 'should' hold a higher job status relative to their wives. When this norm is violated and wives hold the higher status job, negative consequences can follow. Women are disparagingly referred to as having 'married down,' are more likely to be targets of their husbands' aggression, and the risk for divorce increases." The study found "that wives who believed they held higher status positions than their husbands were, indeed, more likely to experience feelings of resentfulness or embarrassment, feeling that their status was decreased by their husband's lower status position, which, in turn, had a negative impact on their marital satisfaction - and even increased the likelihood that they were thinking about divorce."

It is interesting to note that husbands were unaffected by their wives' spillover feelings and only experienced greater dissatisfaction and thoughts about divorce if their wives were outwardly unhappy about their relationship.

The study also showed that when wives felt their husbands provided them with high levels of instrumental support, such as helping with domestic responsibilities, or child and elder care, holding higher status positions than their husbands was not associated with marital instability. This was not the case if their partner simply provided emotional support, suggesting that it is the *tangible* support that husbands provide to higher job status wives that matters more. The researchers suspect that this is true for two reasons: it allows the wife to focus on her career and it denotes respect.

It also helps to be self-aware individually and as part of the couple. Honesty and open communication is critical. Barbara Corcoran, a very successful real estate broker and a host on Shark Tank, notes that the first year her income exceeded her husband's she pretended it was an accounting error. By the time the third-year hit, she was earning more than five times what he was. She said, "When you're a big money earner and your husband isn't, it makes you question how feminine you are. I felt I was less feminine than if I was a supportive wife, or second fiddle. The struggle was as much mine as my husband's."[41]

Her husband has had glory days in his career. He was an FBI agent who had more arrests than anyone, held a top post in the Naval Reserve during the first Persian gulf war, ran his family's real estate company until he sold it, and took a teaching fellowship. Then his title on his business card became "spouse."

They worked out their issues because, as Corcoran notes, her husband had a very strong identity and was successful in his life. When she takes her business personality into the house he forces her to be a partner, not a boss. That (and a lot of therapy), she says, is what keeps her marriage healthy. He won't give her an inch of satisfaction and won't acknowledge her superiority.

It is interesting to note that a study done by the Center for Research on Families at the University of Washington found that the more money the wife makes, the more housework she does in proportion to her husband and it's not nearly as equitable as when both parties are working. There is an association of housework being woman's work. The wives are not going to compound the difficulty by having the husband do more housework.

And, of course, not only do both spouses work in most families today; for some of those couples, both are powerful in their respective careers. Those marriages are built on a mutual understanding of the pressures at work and an appreciation and respect for how much each values his or her career.

Power couple marriages are under tremendous stress if one person is addicted to work. The other spouse can view that work addiction as much of a betrayal as an extramarital affair. In a dual career marriage, each spouse's career will ebb and flow on its own right and the roles each takes in the relationship will ebb and flow with it.

In a Wharton article, *High Powered Women and Supportive Spouses: Who is in Charge, and of What?*[42] couples discussed this dilemma. Gail McGovern worked at AT&T overseeing 10,000 employees and her husband ran a large unit at Hewlett-Packard. They both traveled for work and one of them needed to be home for their daughter. According to McGovern, they had two monster jobs. In the beginning they fought about who got to take a particular work trip and then they instituted the kitchen calendar rule: whoever booked it first got to take the trip. McGovern recalled that during those years her house was always a mess and there was very little cooking, mainly take-out. For both, being there while their daughter was growing up was important and neither of them ever missed one of their daughter's school assemblies, recitals, or parent-teacher conferences.

Power couples and dual career couples learn to keep the relationship going. They prioritize spending time together, outsource childcare and household chores to nannies and family members, communicate with each other, and take the time every day to listen to what the other spouse is saying. They respect each other and their respective contributions.

Francois-Henri Pinault, film actress Selma Hayek's husband wanted her to go back to work after having children. "I don't want you to be deprived of your work. I want to watch it, too. And the world has not seen the best of you yet. So, you cannot stop until some more of your work put out." According to Hayek he really pushed her and told her "Get up on your feet and get out there." She did and said he was right.[43]

In her book, *Couples that Work,*[44] Professor Jennifer Petriglieri writes that her six year research into the lives of 100 dual career couples (from around the world, age range mid-20s to mid-60s and a range of professionals) reveals that they overcome their challenges by directly addressing deeper psychological and social forces, such as struggles for power and control, personal hopes, fears and losses, and assumptions and cultural expectations about the roles partners should play in each other's lives and what it means to have a good relationship or career.

It is a challenge to remain independent and have a life plan with shared life goals. Setting aside time - at least annually - to review the joint life goals and assess where each in the couple is individually, and where they are collectively, can be very powerful and life-changing. Openly discussing financial contributions is important too. (Whose name does an asset go in? Who is contributing what? Who is paying what bill from what income? What is the savings/investment goal? If one spouse owns a business what is to be plowed back into it?)

Belinda Luscombe, editor-at-large for *Time*, in her book, *Marriageology,*[45] asks an interesting question: *What is the point of marriage now*? All the benefits that marriage traditionally offered - sex, children, status, (and, 50 to 60 years ago, for women a provider, for men, a housekeeper) - have all been outsourced. We don't need to get married for any of those things anymore. Marriage has all the buzz now and much less of the purpose, so when people get married, they think, *Wow, I did it*! And then they say, *Wow this is hard.*

According to Luscombe, marriage is a process. Pair bonding and finding a mate, are natural things to do. The entire animal kingdom does that. We, as humans, are one of the rare species that tries to do it forever. For her, marriage is a little bit like learning to write. She could write a bit when she started her career in journalism. And now she is better at it, and it is satisfying to be better at something. She has been married 30 years plus to the same man and, she writes, she is just better at him – better at loving him, better at understanding what he needs, and finds satisfaction in just being good at *him.*

Marriage in many ways is not natural, but it is not natural in the same way that all those fantastic things that we do, like reading and dancing or writing poetry. What's natural about poetry? They are higher-order skills that are worthwhile. She writes that is how she feels about marriage. "It's not something that happens to you. It's something you do. I mean, that's love. Love is not just something that you fall into; it's something you learn to do."

What does all this mean? To me, it means that to be a partner in a successful marriage it is important to know who you are, understand your power, know what you want and know what you expect. At the same time, it is important to make sure that your spouse understands his power, knows what he wants and what he expects. Given those basics, you can develop mutual goals and expectations, and address unconscious biases as they crop up. The key is to communicate, negotiate and discuss your issues (and there will be many) continuously.

# Chapter 3:

# Ageless Wisdom, Intuition and Empathy

Women are said to have superior innate characteristics that men may have, but not at the same level of intensity: ageless wisdom, intuition, and empathy. Why is that? Is it biological? Is it inherent? Can it be learned or improved? Does it matter?

## Ageless Wisdom

> **"Before the moon I am, what a woman is, a woman of power, a woman's power, deeper than the root of trees, deeper than the roots of islands, older than the Making, older than the moon."**
>
> -Ursula K. Le Guin, Tehanu

Women are born knowing certain things. Ageless wisdom is a fundamental thread women have carried and passed down through cultures and generations. It is mysterious and multi-dimensional. As an example, women are not taught how to give birth; they know how to give birth. Women have a deep, intuitive instinct about birth.

Carl Jung introduced the theory of a "collective unconscious" which is innate, not learned. The collective unconscious consists of mythological themes, which projected outside create myths and symbols. The archetypal images are similar for all cultures, common to all people of different ages and races. They appear consistently in mythology, fairy tales, religious traditions, mysteries, and rituals. They have the same psychological content in the East and the West.[46]

Universal predispositions that stem from our ancestral past can be seen in some of our everyday behaviors in several ways. The collective unconscious is often described as a type of innate genetic memory that can be shared by individuals with a common ancestor or history. As an example, the theory of the collective unconscious may explain the fear of snakes and spiders among children, suggesting that the fear could be inborn. In other words, young children may have the "innate wisdom" to avoid dangers like snakes even though they have had no personal experience with snakes.

Jean Shinoda Bolen, a Jungian psychologist concludes that there are seven ancient female archetypes which are "symbolic figures and mythic themes that reside deep in the collective unconscious." Every woman is born with the knowledge of these archetypes. Depending on which goddess is more active within, one woman might be more committed to achieving professional success, while another more fulfilled as a wife and mother. In her book Shonda Bolen teaches women to decide which archetype to cultivate and which ones to overcome so that each woman can become a better "heroine" in her own life story.[47]

Innate feminine wisdom can hide today. Women in the work force flex their masculine muscles and compete with men. Gail Straub, Cofounder and Executive Director of Empowerment Institute, in her book, *"Returning to My Mother's House: Taking Back the Wisdom of the Feminine,"* notes that "no matter where we live, we're encouraged to go toward the masculine or outer qualities, towards our "father's house." That is the world of performance, concrete results, and rational thought. Too often our "mother's house" - female wisdom - is put down. It is not important. It's not useful. Those qualities are deep intuition, emotional intelligence, and the capacity to cultivate an "inner life." Straub calls these inner qualities the "wisdom of the feminine" and when there is balance between the feminine and masculine qualities, women are most content and fulfilled.[48]

Ageless inner wisdom is priceless (and lasts far longer than physical beauty). Tapping into innate wisdom requires inner reflection, trying to connect with nature and its essence, and spending time and sharing experiences with other women, including those of different generations.

## Intuition

> **"A woman knows by intuition, or instinct, what is best for herself."**
>
> -Marilyn Monroe

We have all heard of the power of a woman's intuition and that it is important to listen to our sixth sense, our gut instinct, our inner voice. I knew the day that my mother died that it would be the day of her death hours before it happened. I just sensed it and knew it was important to go to her home. I was right. She died a few hours later.

I have also experienced that gut feeling in business - a meeting that was just not going to go well, a feeling that the mail would bring difficult correspondence. My gut feeling has often been right. When I have ignored it, I have done so at my own peril. So, do women have special powers? What is women's intuition and how can we consciously (not unconsciously) use it in life?

Psychologist Ronald E. Riggio says women's intuitive powers are real and are based on gender differences in nonverbal communication skills.[49] Women as a group are generally better at reading facial expressions of emotions than men are, he says, and therefore they are more likely to pick up on the subtle emotional messages that are sent from others. Women are also better at expressing emotions through their facial expressions, tones of voice, and body language - particularly positive emotions. Men are better at controlling felt emotions and at hiding behind a "poker face."

Riggio says there is also evidence that women are more empathetic than men, more likely to see themselves as empathic, and that makes them more open to others' emotional messages and may add to the perception that women have some special ability to intuit what others are feeling or thinking.

Evolutionary elements may have been involved, selecting out females who had a better ability to decide the needs of children and potential mates. A 2017 study led by the University of Cambridge with collaborators from Australia, France, the Netherlands, and the United States tested whether there were genetic variants associated with cognitive empathy (our ability to be able to understand another person's emotional state just at a glance).[50]

90,000 people were shown different photographs of people's eyes. When asked what they thought that person's mood was, women consistently outperformed men. Katrina Grasby of Australia's Medical Research Institute in Queensland, one of the researchers involved with this study, said the results showed significant differences between females and males but raised questions as to why this was true.

There is also evidence that people can improve their ability to read and send emotional messages. Dr. Mona Lisa Schulz and Dr. Christiane Northrup posit that the female brain today is not our grandmother's brain.[51] It has even more connections and skills. Our lives today are bombarded with greater and greater complexity, so the New Feminine Brain must exaggerate and overdevelop its intuition. Schulz contends that on top of our inborn feminine wiring, women must develop or "sprout" new pathways in our brains - new responses, actions and behaviors - to survive in jobs and careers that require a more male, compartmentalized brain style, and that women's brains have a greater capacity to sprout connections and change "shape" over time. Not only are there more connections in the female brain, those connections can proliferate and change over time in response to stimulation and new, more challenging environments.

When women speak, they use their analytical left brain and their emotional right brain simultaneously. This hyper connectivity between the brain hemispheres makes women more likely to make right brain emotional hunches (i.e. channel intuition) *and* to talk about those emotional hunches using the rational and analytical language of the left brain. Schulz contends that similarly, a woman has an exaggerated capacity to sense stimuli, pain, and health changes in her body and because she is in touch with these right brain-body information nerve highways, she may be more likely to talk about intuition that she gets from her body.

In her book, *How Women Decide: What's True, What's Not and What Strategies Spark the Best Choices,* cognitive scientist Therese Huston contends that scientists find that expert intuitions whether made by men or women are fast, holistic, and unconscious.[52] To be useful, employing intuition requires a lot of practice with clear feedback. She says many people think they have good instincts, but the reality is they have not received immediate or clear feedback on their guesses, so their gut feelings may not come across as accurate as they would like to believe. Women tend to rely on thoughtful, deliberate, and conscious analysis just as often, if not somewhat more often, than men. Compared to men, women have learned to be more accurate at deciphering emotions from others' facial expressions and body language. However, Huston contends this is not about "women's intuition" so much as it is the intuition of whoever happens to be in the subordinate part of the relationship.

Indeed, research suggests that because women have been historically lower in social power, they have spent more time observing and scrutinizing those in power and become more attuned to their nonverbal clues. In a 1985 Harvard study conducted by Sara Snodgrass, male and female students were put in pairs to work together for an hour. Sometimes two women worked together, sometimes two men, and sometimes one man and a woman. Snodgrass varied who was in charge; half the time a man was assigned to be the leader of the team and half the time a woman was assigned to lead.

If women naturally have the upper hand in sensitivity, then we would expect that women would always be stronger at reading nonverbal clues, regardless of who they partnered with and what role they played. But that is not what happened. Snodgrass found that the subordinates - regardless of gender - were better at reading the clues of their leaders, and she concluded that instead of calling it *women's* intuition we should call it *subordinates'* intuition.[53]

One wonders what this means as women are increasingly not playing the subordinate role. Will men become more intuitive? Will both men and women become increasingly intuitive? What impact will that have on family? On the workplace? On society?

## Empathy

> **"When you start to develop your powers of empathy and imagination, the whole world opens up to you."**
>
> – Susan Sarandon

Empathy is defined as the ability to understand and share the feelings of another. ("I feel your pain."). It is not kindness or pity. Empathy is important because it allows us to understand what others are thinking and feeling. This improves our communication skills. With empathy we are better able to respond to others. Positive empathy, or "the ability to share, celebrate, and enjoy others' positive emotions," bolsters individual wellbeing and relationship strength. Connecting with positive people can improve the quality of your life. Empathy is also a (new) leadership skill.

Science shows that women are more empathetic than men. According to a Netherlands research study, "During social interactions we automatically infer motives, intentions, and feelings from bodily cues of others, especially from the eye region of their faces. This cognitive empathetic ability is one of the most important components of social intelligence and is essential for effective social interaction. Females on average outperform males in this cognitive empathy."[54]

Researchers believe the male sex hormone, testosterone, is involved. They found that women with higher testosterone levels are also less empathetic. Administering testosterone to female participants significantly impaired their ability to read the mind from the eyes. Opposite effects (i.e. improvements in cognitive empathy) have been shown after administering the "female-type" peptide hormone oxytocin in healthy young males." In other words, female hormones increase cognitive empathy and male hormones decrease it.

The data in a UCLA research study on the brain activity of people as they reacted to images of pain in others suggests that females are better at feeling another's pain and getting at the feeling that the other person is having. In the study participants lay down in an MRI scanner and viewed a video clip of a human hand, which was either being poked with a syringe or, as a control condition, with a cotton swab. The purpose was to obtain people's immediate reflexive neural responses to the sight of someone else in pain.[55]

The researchers looked at the blood-oxygen-level-dependent (BOLD) signal as a measure of the ratio of oxygenated to non-oxygenated blood and the change in blood flow between the conditions. From that they inferred that an area of the brain is more active in one condition than another. Female participants in the study showed relatively higher activation in the sensory area of the brain associated with pain than their male counterparts.

Dr. Marco Iacobini, a leader in the study, notes, "One way I understand your pain is that in my brain I mimic what would happen to me if I felt the pain myself." And in females, the area that mimics the pain of others shows a bigger response. That is an indication that women's responses are more empathetic; they are feeling other people's pain more than the male participants are. He believes that one of the paper's main contributions is that it lets us understand the mechanism that creates this difference in empathy between females and males. Females may be more empathetic because they really understand your predicament, your emotional state. They feel it almost under their skin.

Empathy is in the "mommy brain" too. Current evidence shows that pregnancy changes the brain on a physical, cellular level. A woman's brain changes are an example of neuroplasticity, the process in which the brain changes through life by reorganizing connections in response to the stimulation of new experiences and neurogenesis, the process of growth that allows for new learning.[56]

A 2016 study in Nature Neuroscience found that even two years after pregnancy, women had gray matter changes in regions involved in social cognition or the ability to empathetically understand what is going on in the mind of another person. One theory behind this is that the changes may have an evolutionary benefit to strengthen the communication between a mother and her infant, which improves a mother's ability to help the child first understand the outside world and then learn how to make sense of it.[57]

Empathy may also affect career choice. A University of Cambridge (England) study investigated the disparity between male and female career choices and asked if our brain type can explain the gender gap in STEM subjects and careers. According to the researchers, "Rather than seeing gender per se as being the dividing factor... it is one's ability to empathize and systemize that attracts or repels people from entering into STEM subjects and embarking on careers in this domain. It is true that many more females are categorized as empathizers and many more males as systemizers, which may explain the gender disparity. Empathizing is the internal drive to identify with another person's emotions and thoughts and respond to them with appropriate emotions and actions; systemizing is the cognitive ability to identify the underlying rules that govern the behavior of the system."[58]

It turns out that too much empathy can have negative aspects. Robin Stern, associate director of the Yale Center for Emotional Intelligence points out that empathy is an essential ingredient for building intimacy in relationships. When someone feels seen and heard by you they begin to trust you. This can also have a downside, especially if you become so consumed by another's feelings that you neglect your own feelings and needs. Those who regularly prioritize others' emotions over their own are more susceptible to experiencing anxiety or low-level depression.[59]

A four-year study of Dutch physicians shows that female doctors show more empathy than male doctors. They ask their patients more questions, including questions about emotions and feelings, and they spend more time talking to their patients. Although this may make them better doctors, it may also impact their health. The female doctors were at a greater risk of burnout and when someone feels burned out, she is exhausted, emotionally depleted, cynical, and detached. Doctors with burn out make more mistakes and are less likely to answer patients' questions or fully discuss their treatment options. As they burnout, they show less empathy for others (compassion fatigue).[60]

Is empathy a new, critical leadership skill? Feminine qualities, such as emotional intelligence and organizational skills matter today in the workforce. English psychologist Mary Sherry states that "Modern women finally seem confident in their own skin and no longer feel they have to play hard ball to be accepted. Instead of being driven by demons and outdated management values, they have learned to play the success game by making the most of their intellect. That means using the rational side of their brain to solve problems, and then relying on their feminine wiles to hammer home the message. Instead of speaking in Klingon, women now come across as being rational creatures with the added skills of both empathy and cooperation. In addition, they realize that their triumph relies on other people's efforts. It is not a denial of the self but a celebration of being able to use both sides of the brain. Trying to be a man in an evolving world will only hinder a woman's chance of career advancement."[61]

Author Barbara Bowes, a leader in the field of human resources, believes empathy is the new leadership skill. It is a critical skill to have in a global world because our workforce is becoming increasingly diverse and leaders now need to build cross agency and cross border relationships, be sensitive to intercultural nuances and be effective at aligning goals between a wide variety of social groups, all with different goals, strategies, and protocols.[62]

The US-based Center for Creative Leadership conducted research on leadership traits for today's world. Gathering input from the employees of 6,731 leaders in 38 countries, they found empathy is positively related to job performance. The results showed a successful leader in today's world needs to be more "person-focused" or empathetic. Empathetic leaders were found to show interest in their employees' needs, were willing to help with personal issues, and demonstrated compassion - interest in the hopes and dreams of their employees. Being empathetic allows leaders to "know" employees and predict how individuals will respond to their directions and decisions, especially those that will directly impact them. It enables leaders to develop strategies that will help them effectively sell their changes and management ideas.[63]

One wonders, however, if there might be a dark side to empathy. Is it easier to strive for success when the only thing in your vision is the goal you are aiming for? Is it more difficult to do so when you are aware of how your efforts might impact others along the way? Can empathy thus hinder women in the workplace?

As the gender balance at home is shifting, does empathy add pressure to the woman because she is more aware of the unexpressed concerns of her husband and children?

As we know, it is impossible to please everyone, even some of the time. Perhaps empathy is something to be made aware of and managed so that women can utilize it to their advantage, rather than fall victim to it.

## Chapter 4:

# Women's Power Through Direct and Indirect Influence

**Never underestimate the influence you have on others.**

*- Laurie Buchanan Ph.D.*

The power of a woman's influence is not new; in fact, it has always existed. It is easy to think of power as direct. It is harder to step back and ponder the importance of power when it is indirect. The indirect influence can, in fact, be more powerful than overt influence. The traditional female influence remains at home in the family and is now also in the workforce, in politics, and in global leadership. Women's influence has impacted societal codes of conduct, religion, social reform, and philanthropy.

## Indirect Influence through the power of nurturing.

Women have an instinct to make sure that those they love (spouse/significant other, parents, children, and grandchildren) are supported, safe, and taken care of. Women who do not have children still have the instinct to nurture. Women who work and women who do not work have an instinct to nurture. The power of nurture is creative and transformative. It has a profound impact on the life of the nurturer and on the lives of those that the nurturer touches.

Distinguished Professor Shelley E. Taylor posits that females of all species, including humans, have been the primary caretakers of offspring, and so it stands to reason that their responses to stress have evolved to include a measure of protection for children.[64]

The stress response, "fight or flight" is a male perspective based on power and aggression. The "tend and befriend" response to stress is a female response. Human survival has been based on group living. From an evolutionary standpoint humans would not have survived had they not evolved ways of coping with stress that involved the protection of offspring from harm and group living to fend off threats and predators. A female stands a better chance of protecting herself and her offspring if she tends to those offspring and enlists the help of the social group for protection as well. Under conditions of threat, women tend to offspring to ensure their survival and affiliate with others for joint protection and comfort.

Taylor backs up the "tend and friend" theory by presenting thirty studies with thirty unanimous conclusions that women fall back on systems of social support in times of crisis. Included in her book are studies about support groups suffering terminal illness that showed women who participated in these groups lived longer than women who received only medical care.

Generational nurturing happens in many families. Oprah Winfrey lived her early years with her grandmother on her farm. "I was a child born out of wedlock," she says, "and my mother moved to the North. I was left with my grandmother. It probably saved my life. It is the reason why I am where I am today. My grandmother gave me the foundation for success that I was allowed to continue to build upon. My grandmother taught me to read, and that opened the door to all kinds of possibilities for me. I loved books so much as a child. They were my outlet to the world."[65]

## Influences on Moral Codes of Conduct.

From the women in Arthurian England to the Flappers, women have had tremendous influence on moral codes of conduct.

Analyzing the compilation of Arthurian legends from England and France published in 1485, scholar Janet Jesmok investigated the importance of women as the "wise, sometimes prescient voices of judgment" and found that from minor figures to important female characters, women assessed and judged in matters of social and courtly behavior, chivalry, love, and morality. Jesmok argues that women's influence over codes of chivalry and correct behavior gave them unique power. The awareness of the code, in combination with the lack of a parallel code designed to regulate feminine behavior, opened a space of feminine influence at the very heart of the masculine chivalric enterprise.[66]

The French journalist, Alexis De Tocqueville wrote at the end of Volume II of his 19th Century essays on *Democracy in America*, "If I were asked to what the singular prosperity and growing strength of that people ought mainly to be attributed, I should reply: *To the superiority of their women.*"[67]

De Tocqueville stated that his interest in analyzing American women arose from the fact that no free communities ever existed without morals and morals were the work of women. Consequently, whatever affected the condition of women, their habits and their opinions, had great political importance. "The American woman is full of reliance on her own strength because she is taught to be firm in her virtue and educated about the realities of life from a young age. As a result, if she does not abandon herself to evil, at least she knows that it exists, and she is remarkable rather for purity of manners than for chastity of mind."[68]

In the 1920s American women influenced and changed the moral code of the time in ways De Tocqueville hadn't imagined. The roaring 1920s Flappers were a generation of women who were experiencing more freedom in their personal lives and had new ideas about how to live.[69] World War I ended in 1918. The Spanish flu epidemic of 1918 killed 20-40 million people. These events inspired in young people a feeling that life was short and could end at any moment. The 1920s were a new beginning. With the 1920s came the 19th Amendment, giving women the right to vote.

After-World War I, women joined the workforce in large numbers, and exerted their influence as consumers, making women's fashion magazines - *Vogue*, *The Queen*, and *Harper's Bazaar* - very popular. The Flappers rebelled against the Victorian image of womanhood, cut their hair short, rejecting the traditional requirement that women wore their hair long, wore heavy make-up, and changed fashion for the ease of movement (dancing). Flappers flaunted their sexuality, drove cars, smoked cigarettes (previously only done by men), drank alcohol, used slang, and shocked their parents. Unlike their mothers and grandmothers, Flappers tended to go to high school and college.

A leading psychologist, G. Stanley Hall, warned, "Without womanly ideals the female character is threatened with disintegration," and older suffragettes, who had fought hard for the right of women to vote, viewed Flappers as vapid. However, Dorothy Dubar Bromley, a noted liberal author at the time, described Flappers as "truly modern," "New Style" feminists who "admit that a full life calls for marriage and children," and also "are moved by an inescapable inner compulsion to be individuals in their own right."

With the Flappers women began competing in the business world, obtaining more financial independence (and therefore other kinds of independence) from men.

## Indirect Influence through music:

Music has always been a powerful way woman influence culture and society, and while the Flappers were creating one new, liberated lifestyle, women's blues singers in the 1920s were creating another - a different model of black women - more assertive, sexy, sexually aware, independent, realistic, complex, and alive.

In her book, *Blues Legacies and Black Feminism,* American political activist and author, Angela Yvonne Davis notes that black women were the first to record blues music in the United States. The black blues singers produced a vast body of musical texts and a rich cultural heritage.[70]

Like most forms of popular music, African American blues lyrics talk about love. Davis states that what is distinctive about the blues, however, particularly in relation to other American popular music forms of the 1920s and 1930s, is their intellectual independence and representational freedom.

Emerging after the decades following the abolition of slavery, the blues gave musical expression to the new social and sexual realities encountered by African Americans as free women and men. The status of their personal relationships had been revolutionized. For the first time in the history of the African presence in North America, masses of black women and men were able to make autonomous decisions regarding the sexual partnerships into which they entered. Sexuality was therefore one of the most tangible domains in which emancipation was acted upon and through which its meanings were expressed.

Women blues singers were performing as professional artists and attracting large audiences with revival-like gatherings. Gertrude “Ma” Rainey and Bessie Smith, two of the most widely known female blues singers, preached about sexual love, and in doing so, they articulated a collective experience of freedom, giving voice to the most powerful evidence there was for many black people that slavery no longer existed.

They were articulating something else as well. In Bessie Smith’s rendition of “Sam Jones’ Blues” (1923), she satirically accentuates the contrast between the dominant cultural construction of marriage and the economic independence black women were compelled to assume for their sheer survival:

*Sam Jones left his lovely wife just to step around*
*Came back home 'bout a year;*
*lookin' for his high brown*
*Went to his accustomed door*
*and he knocked his knuckles sore*
*His wife she came, but to his shame,*
*she knew his face no more.*
*Sam said, "I'm your husband, dear."*
*But she said, "Dear that's strange to hear.*
*You ain't talking to Mrs. Jones,*
*you speaking to Miss Wilson now."*
*...Was a time you could have walked right in*
*and called this place your home sweet home.*
*But for now, it's all mine for all time,*
*I'm free and livin' all alone"*

Davis argues that representations of love and sexuality in women's blues often blatantly contradicted mainstream assumptions regarding women and being in love. They also challenged the notion that women's place was in the domestic sphere. Before the second wave feminist movement of the 1970s the performances of classic blues women, especially Bessie Smith's, were also one of the few cultural spaces to establish a public discourse about domestic violence and abuse.

Davis contends that's because blues as a genre never adhered to the boundaries separating the private sphere from the public sphere. Naming issues - like violence against women - that posed a threat to the physical or psychological wellbeing of the individual was a central function of the blues, and as a result, women's blues made it culturally possible to take a stance in opposition. By naming the problem of male violence, women's blues ushered it out of the shadows of domestic life, where society had kept it hidden and beyond public or political scrutiny.

The lives of many of the blues women in the 1920s resembled those of the fearless women memorialized in their songs. In sum, they were role models for thousands of their sisters to whom they delivered messages that defied the male dominance encouraged by mainstream culture. Blues women openly challenged the gender politics implicit in traditional cultural representations of marriage and love relationships. By refusing to romanticize relationships and instead expose the stereotypes and explore the contradictions in the relationships, they redefined women's "place," forging and memorializing images of tough, resilient, and independent women who were neither afraid of their own vulnerability nor of defending their right to be respected as autonomous human beings.

The profound impact of music on culture is still happening today. The "Queen of Pop," Madonna, and her music have had a profound impact on American culture. Historian professor Glen Jeansoonne said, "Madonna freed Americans from their inhibitions and made them feel good about having fun."[71]

American feminist, academic and social critic Camille Paglia from the University of the Arts, called Madonna a "true feminist" and noted that "she exposes the Puritanism and suffocating ideology of American feminism which is stuck in an adolescent whining mode." According to Paglia, "Madonna has taught young women to be fully female and sexual while still exercising total control over their lives."

## Indirect Influence Through Role Models:

We are all role models and we have all been influenced by role models. Groundbreaking women inspire others to act. Billie Jean King fought for gender equality in tennis and paved the way for Venus and Serena Williams. Marie Curie, the physicist and chemist was the first female recipient of The Nobel Prize. Maya Angelou, the poet, and civil rights activist was a black woman who expressed herself openly and honestly. Her activism has impacted political leaders, entertainers, artists, and game changers. A young woman looking at Billie Jean King, or the Williams sisters, Marie Curie or Maya Angelou can ask herself the question, "If she can do it, why can't I?"[72]

The late Ruth Bader Ginsburg was a powerful role model to young women. She was tough as nails, very happily married, a mother and a grandmother. Ginsburg changed the way the world is for American women. She was a mother before starting at Harvard Law School, where she was one of only a few women in the class. She transferred to Columbia Law School and graduated (joint) first in the class. She taught at Rutgers Law School and Columbia Law School. She was the first Jewish woman and the second woman to serve on the United States Supreme Court. Among her many accomplishments, Ginsburg spent much of her legal career as an advocate for gender equality and women's rights, winning many arguments before the United States Supreme Court.[73]

Part of the power of role models is based on what psychologist Shelley Taylor refers to as "positive illusions," people's tendency to view themselves as above average, and to hold a positive view of their abilities or their likelihood of success in the future. Taylor and her colleagues suggest these illusions (when not extreme) are adaptive and essential for mental health. As an example, if I believe getting an A (instead of a B or a C) in a course is a real possibility, I am more likely to put in a greater effort, and in so doing I am more likely to get a better grade than if I did not assume doing well in the course was possible for me.[74]

Research suggests role models can be influential. One report analyzed the role of female politicians, noting that "over time, the more that women politicians are made visible by national news coverage, the more likely adolescent girls are to want to be politically active." In addition, "Where candidates are visible due to viable campaigns for high-profile offices, girls report increased anticipated political involvement."[75]

A recent theory suggests role models serve three functions: inspirational, potential, and behavioral. Using Hillary Clinton as an example as a possible role model, the woman would ask herself four questions, by looking up to Clinton do you get the feeling that if she can do it, you can do it? Does she model how you need to think or behave to become a successful politician? Does she inspire? From watching her do you get the sense that becoming a politician is a rewarding and fulfilling career for a woman like you?

Of course, a role model does not have to be famous. It can be someone you work with, another mother at the school, someone you have met and do not know well. Role models stand out because they are authentic. Your mother or grandmother may be a powerful role model. Nina Tassler, former CEO Entertainment chairman who oversaw 200 programs including *The Big Bang Theory* and *Madam Secretary*, credits her positive attitude and her determination to her mother. She wrote a book, *What I Told My Daughter*, which describes the important role mothers play in empowering their daughters. Her mother revealed her strengths and flaws equally and she was very much influenced by that. She came to understand that we will all face challenges and obstacles. We will all fail, and we will all have success. But a lot of it will be character building. And it will not deter us from wanting to achieve, to strive, and to be successful.[76]

In 1963 her parents took over a camp business from her grandparents and turned it into a progressive co-educational, interracial camp for kids from all over the world. It was an important cause for both her parents. Three days later before the camp officially opened, the dining room burned to the ground. Hundreds of kids were about to arrive by bus. She saw her mother's face, first tears streaming and then the tears dried. Her mother went back to the house, sat down, and figured out what she was going to do because she had no choice. In three days, ten buses full of campers were going to arrive. As a solution her mother turned the social hall into the dining room. Tassler notes that everything her mother planned, dreamed, and hoped for went up in flames. She saw her courage and conviction and her strategy to put together the pieces and to solve the problem. That influenced her later in life. Understanding the ability to pick herself up, be resilient, embrace a failure, and turn it into an opportunity was one of the greatest gifts her mother gave her.

A workplace study shows that daughters of employed mothers across 29 countries are 1.21 times more likely to be employed, are 1.20 times more likely to supervise others and have higher annual earnings.[77] than daughters of unemployed mothers.

Role models are an effective way to encourage women to make different choices. A study by Kapersky Lab revealed that a lack of feminine role models in STEM (Science, Technology, Engineering and Mathematics) careers discourage more than a third of young women from choosing careers in STEM fields such as cyber security, programming, and research and development. The concept "seeing is believing" works. When women see other women in roles, they find it easier to imagine themselves in these roles and are more likely to put themselves forward. When women see women in leadership positions, they are more likely to speak up for themselves. Female students are more likely to choose a major in STEM when they are assigned a female professor instead of a male one.[78]

When men see women do it, they know it is possible for women to do it. In a study during a women's leadership project in India, they found that men who had been exposed to a minimum of two female village leaders were more likely to vote for women themselves.

It is important to understand that we are all role models for those who watch us. Taking that seriously can be inspirational and life changing for our daughters, granddaughters, employees, and others whose lives we touch.

## Indirect Influence through Consumerism

It is no secret women are "born to shop." In 1929 home economist and marketing expert Christine Frederick published *Selling Mrs. Consumer*, a popular book that instructed manufacturers and advertisers how to pitch products to women.[79]

Women have, of course, always shopped. As far back as the 18th century women bartered and bought goods. The self-conscious identification of women with consumerism after 1890 was linked to the growing sense that consumption involved not only the purchase of goods but a way of life. Shopping was transformed from a functional activity into a form of leisure. Show rooms, window displays, and mirrors appeared, as did a range of services designed for women - from restrooms to restaurants, package delivery, and credit. Women's magazines founded from 1885 to 1910 (*Ladies Home Journal, McCall's, Delineator, Woman's Home Companion, Pictorial Review and Good Housekeeping*) fostered the culture of consumption. Magazine layouts reinforced women readers as consumers, placing ads strategically. By the 1910s advertisers and manufacturers began to see the woman as the chief purchasing agent for the family, buying most of the household's food, clothing, appliances, and other goods.[80]

It even extended to automobiles, which had always been marketed to men. By the late 1920s advertisers began to produce cars in a multitude of colors, urging women to match their cars to their frocks. Radio manufacturers housed vacuum tubes and wires inside mahogany cases to complement living room decor. Smoking was encouraged with slogans such as "Reach for a Lucky instead of a sweet," appealing to a woman's desire to be slender.[81]

The power of the female consumer has only gotten stronger over time and today, women drive the world economy. Globally, women control about $20 trillion in annual consumer spending. Women drive 70-80 percent of all consumer purchasing through a combination of their buying power and influence.[82]

Labor Department data on how singles spend their money offer some insight into women's spending. Single women making $50,000 to $69,990 spend about the same amount on a vehicle purchase as comparable men but allocate more money to new vehicles and not to used ones. Women also spend more on personal care products, services, and on pets. Single women spend more on education than men do and spend less on alcohol than men do. Morgan Stanley points to women's affinity for the off price "treasure hunt" experience, which could include secondhand apparel, home goods, and furniture. Women take purchasing environment-friendly products more into account than men do. Women look for brands to be inclusive and relatable before settling on a purchase.[83]

Women are doing more than using their wallets to influence big brand decisions. Women are leading boardroom meetings and playing a bigger role in corporate decision making. Jamie Gilpin points out that brands are now embracing a lot of qualities we have deemed traditionally female - transparency, honesty, empathy. What is more, because women have traditionally had a harder time raising venture funds, women are now becoming investors themselves and changing the way partners identify which businesses to invest in. Gilpin notes that women make up 30% of all angel investors today, and research shows a female partner is more likely to invest in a female founder.[84]

Brands are listening to this. The founder of Jiffy Lube noticed that more women than men brought their cars in for an oil change. He made sure each location had a clean bathroom, hot coffee waiting, and racks of women's magazines so that the woman who brought the car in and waited would consider herself welcome and come back the next month.

Madewell ran campaigns featuring older women to highlight the versatility of their clothing, which had traditionally been targeted to younger women. Ariel, a consumer products company in India, started a "Share the Load" campaign, urging men to answer, "Why is laundry only a woman's job?"[85]

A UBS Family Office Solutions Study released in 2020, *Matriarchs on the Rise,* reports that there are several demographic tailwinds that will continue the growing trend of the power of the female consumer. Forty percent of women make more money than their husbands (almost a four-fold increase since the 1960s). Women's workforce participation continues to grow, and they now hold 52% of all management, professional and related positions in the United States, and women now make up the majority of both graduates from undergraduate programs and advanced degrees.

In addition, the UBS report indicates that there is a high likelihood women will end up managing their estates by themselves at some point in time because women in heterosexual relationships outlive their husbands by five years and the divorce rate continues to be over 50% and is rising for couples over 50 years of age.

All this purchasing power means that women have and will continue to have a significant impact on the consumer market.

## Direct and Indirect Influence through Philanthropy:

Throughout history women have been role models in demonstrating how philanthropic power can influence community and society. Clara Barton established what is known today as the American Red Cross. Helen Keller and Anne Sullivan established the American Foundation for the Blind in 1887. Jane Addams established Hull House, the first settlement house in the United States in 1899 and received the Nobel Peace Prize in 1931 for her work, the first woman to receive that honor.[86] Abby Aldrich Rockefeller cofounded the Museum of Modern Art in 1929 and during her lifetime gave her time, leadership, and financial resources to the museum. Her grandson, Rodman Rockefeller noted, "For her to accomplish what she did must have seemed really amazing at the time. She lifted us from a narrow definition of life to a lot more fun in life, at the same time keeping this very constructive sense of obligation, this sense that there are things to be done and worlds to conquer and places to make improvements."[87]

The trend continues to the present. As Patricia Sellers, Editor at Large for *Fortune*, notes[88] for most of her life Oprah Winfrey donated 10% of her income to charitable causes. In later years this was channelled through the Oprah Winfrey Foundation, which focused on education (most visibly in support of historically black colleges and universities in the United States and Africa). In 2002 she endowed the new Boarding School for African Women. In her Academy of Achievement interview, she stated, "When you educate a woman, you set her free. Had I not had the books and education in Mississippi, I would have believed that is all there was. I don't think you ever stop giving. It's not just about being able to write a check. It's about being able to touch somebody's life. It's being able to make a child see the light in him or herself."

Women collaborate, and collaboration is power in philanthropy. *Women and Giving*, a Rockefeller Philanthropy Advisors Roadmap, notes that women donors often develop their giving strategy around relationships. Outwardly focused, they collaborate, communicate, engage, involve, understand, adapt, and, most importantly, build bridges to different individuals and groups. Their aim: to serve multiple purposes while sustaining or even strengthening relationships.

That is why the "giving circle," a form of charitable collective where people pool small amounts of money in order to make a larger impact, is especially popular among women. According to a 2017 report by the Collective Giving Research group, which was supported by the Women's Philanthropy Institute at Indiana University, the amount of money in giving circles, most of which are fueled by women, has tripled over the last decade, with an estimated $1.29 billion being granted overall.[89] Of the 1,600 publicly identifiable giving groups around the country polled, the average group size was 116 members. Industrywide at least 150,000 people have tried this format, 70% had women as a majority of membership and nearly 50% were women only. Grants were not just for major charities or community foundations. Most of the groups were built locally and gave locally, covering issues such as human services, women and girl equality and education.

The trend for collaborative giving by women for women has been energized by "women's funds" - organizations that award grants to non-profits and programs benefiting women. According to a 2019 Women's Philanthropy

Institute survey of 183 women's funds, three of the funds' prime goals were creating social change, advancing gender equity and equality, and driving the potential for far-reaching social impact. Many women's funds go beyond grant-making to achieve that impact by engaging in activities such as relationship building, partnerships, and policy advocacy.

Women's funds demonstrate a unique model of philanthropy: women investing in women, not just to benefit those women but also their children, families, communities, and society as a whole. While they have been most successful at achieving local level change, their collaborative partnerships and policy advocacy have the potential to effect social change on a grander scale, particularly given that they plan to continue and expand these collaborations.

At the higher end, in 2005 Ambassador Swanee Hunt and her sister, Helen LaKelly Hunt. founded a global funding initiative, Women Moving Millions.[90] They sought to build a global collective of committed, purposeful women making unprecedented gifts of $1 million or more for the advancement of women and girls. In 2020 alone its members have committed over $680 million and are funding many initiatives, using the power of their voices and influence to inspire others to invest with a gender lens.

## Direct Influence Through Social Reform

Just as it has fueled their philanthropy, the innate power of collaboration has enabled women to exert influence over societal change for more than a century, as a result of their involvement in social, education, and prison reform, as well as movements for suffrage and labor rights.

The Women's Trade Union League in 1903 drew together educated women reformers (mostly white, Protestant and native-born) and young women workers (many of them immigrant Jews, Italians and Irish) to improve factory wages, working conditions, and hours.[91] This cross-class women's network deepened with the uprisings of young women garment workers that began in New York in 1909 and then spread into other cities. Middle class and affluent supporters of women's suffrage (including college students and wealthy socialites) saw these strikes as an opportunity to win working women to the suffrage cause. Forming what the press called "mink brigades," affluent supporters marched alongside young immigrant women on picket lines in a largely successful attempt to reduce the high rates of police brutality.

After the 1911 Triangle Shirtwaist Fire, Frances Perkins (the future U.S. Secretary of Labor under Franklin Roosevelt) of the National Consumers League and Pauline Newman (a former Triangle employee and Women's Trade Union activist) were appointed as investigators for the New York State Factory Investigating Committee (FIC), positions they used to educate powerful politicians about the conditions under which working women labored.

Over the next three years the New York FIC and sister organizations pushed through a dramatically expanded regulatory structure for factory labor, including laws that empowered state commissioners of labor, banned the labor of children under age 14, and required inspection of elevators and fireproof devices. After the war, President

Wilson established a permanent Women's Bureau in the U.S. Department of Labor to investigate women's working conditions.

When feminists and unions worked together, both benefitted. Labor gained when it realized women's issues were crucial for the advancement of the working class, and the women's movement was strengthened when its membership and agenda crossed class lines.[92]

## Direct Influence Through Activism

The power of activism can have world-changing consequences. The activist women who obsessively achieved their goals and created positive change were driven, creative, thorough, and thoughtful. Their journeys were not smooth or linear. Despite the obstacles they faced (jail, public humiliation, litigation, direct attacks by the press and respected institutions, unemployment, poverty), they strategically forged onward at the peril of themselves and their families. Margaret Sanger trail blazed the fight for reproductive rights. Rachel Carson took on the chemical companies and paved the way for conservation and environmentalism. Rosa Parks was a catalyst for the civil rights movement in the United States. Each of these women was complicated and each of their goals were mixed. Each had passion, creativity, drive, and the stamina to bring the result they set their minds on to completion and each changed our world forever.

## Margaret Sanger and Reproductive Rights

> **"A woman must not accept; she must challenge. She must be awed by that which has been built up around her; she must reverence that woman in her which struggles for expression."**
>
> -Margaret Sanger

In 1912 Margaret Sanger[93] became a visiting nurse on New York City's lower east side and tended to Jewish and Italian immigrant women at a time when The Comstock Law made birth control illegal. Nursing women back to health after botched abortions, she began her lifelong commitment to help women escape the poverty, illnesses, and death that were caused by having too many pregnancies.

In 1914 she started her own paper called "The Woman Rebel" and, defying the Comstock Law, promised to publish all the information she could about birth control. She was arrested. In the six weeks she was given to prepare her defense she wrote a book on birth control, illustrating the common forms of birth control available. Her book was published in 13 different languages and started the birth control movement.

In 1916, with a $50 contribution from a woman who had heard her speak she opened the country's first birth control clinic in Brooklyn New York. She was arrested ten days later and sentenced to 30 days in jail. In 1918 she won a major legal victory. Doctors (but not nurses) would be allowed to prescribe birth control when it was medically indicated. In 1917 she cofounded *The Birth Control Review*, the first scientific journal devoted to birth control, and became its editor.

She clashed with the Catholic Church on the issue of birth control. Pointing to the 2,000 abortions in the United States every year, she wrote, "The question is not whether family limitation should be practiced. The question is whether it is to be attained by normal, scientific birth control methods or by the abnormal, often dangerous, surgical operation. *Birth Control or Abortion, which shall it be*?"

In 1921 Sanger founded the American Birth Control League which embraced global issues such as slowing world population growth, disarmament and ending world famine. Its founding principles were: "We hold that children should be (1) conceived in love; (2) born of the mother's conscious desire; (3) And only begotten under conditions which render possible the heritage of health. Therefore, we hold that every woman must possess the power and freedom to prevent conception, except when these conditions can be satisfied."

In 1923 she opened the Birth Control Clinical Research Program in New York City, which dispensed contraceptives to women under licensed medical supervision and studied the effect of contraception on women's health in order to broaden the interpretation of the Comstock Law and allow women to use contraceptives for health reasons.

In 1936 significant legal progress was made when the US Supreme Court ordered a sweeping liberalization of federal Comstock Laws as applied to the importing of contraceptive devises. The opinion fell short of finding the Comstock Laws unconstitutional but did find that birth control could no longer be classified as obscene. It took 30 more years for the Comstock Laws to be struck down.

While in her 70s Sanger drove the research and development of the pill. Sanger wanted something women could control on their own and hide if necessary, that was modern and scientific and would work. She started the search for an oral contraceptive in 1951. With funding from International Harvester heiress Katharine Dexter McCormick (an elderly woman who was one of the first women graduates of MIT), Sanger recruited researcher Gregory Pincus to develop an oral contraceptive. Pincus recruited Dr John Rock (an obstetrician) to assist. The first "pill" (known as Enovid) was approved for contraception in 1960. (It is interesting to note that they wanted to be cautious and chose to ask for approval of the pill to regulate the menstrual cycle and had a warning on the bottle "warning: prevents pregnancy.") Sanger died in 1966 at age 86.

## Rachel Carson: Activist for Conservation and the Environment

Rachel Carson's[94] ground-breaking book, *Silent Spring*, created a new public awareness that nature was vulnerable to human intervention and proposed that at times technological progress was so at odds with natural processes that it had to be curtailed. The threats Carson outlined were the contamination of the food chain, cancer, genetic damage, and the death of entire species.

Environmentalism, and the need to regulate industry to protect the environment was born.

Her path to *Silent Spring* was not a direct one. She began her career as an aquatic and nature writer in the 1950s, writing bestselling books about the sea and the interconnectedness of nature and all living things. She explained the shore as an *ecosystem*, a word most had never heard of.

*The Silent Spring* came from research she did as a result of a civic campaign calling attention to the consequences of the insecticide aerial spraying programs of DDT, the most powerful pesticide the world had ever known. Developed in 1939, DDT was important in World War II when it was used to clear the Pacific Islands of malaria-causing insects for U.S. troops. Its inventor won the Nobel Prize. Those decrying the inhuman consequences of DDT called upon Carson to help.

Her research spanned four years. *Silent Spring* appeared in the New Yorker in three parts in 1962 and then as a book. She showed that everything was connected to everything else and in the book's most famous Chapter, "A Fable for Tomorrow" depicted a nameless American town where all life - from fish to birds to apple blossoms to children - had been "silenced" by the insidious effects of DDT.

Carson's message reach was broad and powerful. She made it clear she was not calling for the elimination of helpful pesticides but was instead interested in encouraging responsible and carefully managed use with an awareness of the chemicals' impact on the entire ecosystem. In *Silent Spring* she concludes her section on DDT not by urging a total ban, but by advising spraying as little as possible to limit the development of resistance.

She was attacked by the U.S. chemical industry, which charged her with gross distortions unsupported by scientific evidence. Testifying before Congress, she backed up her book with 55 pages of notes and a list of experts who had read and approved her manuscript. Because of Carson's work, DDT was heavily scrutinized by the government and eventually banned.

Carson's legacy was making the public aware that nature was vulnerable to human intervention.

## Rosa Parks and the Civil Rights Movement

On December 1, 1955, in Montgomery, Alabama, Rosa Parks[95] disobeyed bus driver James F. Blake's order to give up her seat in the "colored section" of the bus to a white passenger, after the bus's white-only section was filled. Parks, a seamstress at a local department store, was also the Secretary of the Montgomery Chapter of the National Association for the Advancement of Colored People (NAACP). Others had resisted bus segregation before her. The NAACP believed in Parks they had found the strongest candidate to bring to court to challenge her arrest for civil disobedience in violating the segregation laws of Alabama.

Those who wrote about Parks described her as "quiet." However, when the Library of Congress opened the Rosa Parks Collection featuring her personal writings and political documents in 2016, the collection clearly showed that Rosa Parks was a life-long activist.

As a young woman, she wrote, "I talked and talked of everything I know about the white man's inhuman treatment of the Negro."

She recalled her elementary school days when white students took the bus and black students walked to school as a time of awakening. "The bus was among the first ways I realized there was a black world and a white world."

When the Ku Klux Klan marched down the street in front of her house, she said her grandfather stood at the front door with a shotgun. When she was bullied by white children, she fought back physically. "As far back as I remember," she said, "I could never think in terms of accepting physical abuse without some form of retaliation if possible."

She married Raymond Parks, a barber who was an activist for the Scottsboro boys (a group of black men falsely accused of raping a white woman.) She received her high school diploma in 1933 at time when less than 7% of African Americans held a high school diploma. In 1943 she joined the Montgomery Chapter of the NAACP and became the branch's secretary. In 1944, after investigating the gang rape of Recy Taylor, a black woman, she helped organize "The Committee for Equal Justice of Recy Taylor," a strong campaign for equal justice.

Her rides on the integrated trolley opened her eyes again. She became a seamstress and secretary to a liberal white couple, Clifford and Virginia Durr, who sponsored her attendance at the Highlander Folk School in Tennessee, an education center for activism in worker's rights and racial equality. She was mentored by Septima Clark, known for organizing.

In 1955 Emmett Till, a black teenager was murdered for flirting with a white woman. Four days before she refused to give up her seat on the bus, Parks attended a mass meeting at Dexter Avenue Baptist Church in Montgomery that addressed the Till case, as well as the murder of activist George W. Lee and the murder of Lamar Smith. At that meeting she learned of the acquittal of the men who had murdered Till.

Four days later she refused to give up her seat on the bus. In her autobiography, *My Story*, she wrote "People always say that I didn't give up my seat because I was tired, but that isn't true. I was not old, although some people have an image of me as being old then. I was forty-two. No, the only tired I was, was tired of giving in."

She was arrested and charged with violating the segregation law of the Montgomery City code. The local Chapter of the NAACP, the Pullman Porters' Union and the Durrs bailed her out of jail that night.

Parks was found guilty at trial, fined $10 plus $4 in court costs. She appealed and challenged the legality of social racial segregation. In a 1992 NPR interview Parks said, "I did not want to be mistreated. I did not want to be deprived of a seat I had paid for. It was just time... there was opportunity for me to take a stand to express the way I felt about being treated in that manner. I had not planned to get arrested. I had plenty to do without having to end up in jail. But when I had to face that decision, I didn't hesitate to do so because I felt we had endured that too long. The more we gave in, the more we complied with that kind of treatment, the more oppressive it became."

A bus boycott was organized in protest of Parks' arrest. A new organization, Montgomery Improvement Association (MIA) was formed to lead the boycott effort. The first President, Martin Luther King Jr.(who was young, not well known at the time, and a minister of the Dexter Avenue Baptist Church) was elected. The boycott continued for 381 days. Montgomery repealed its law requiring segregation on public buses after the US Supreme Court Case, Browder v. Gale ruled it unconstitutional.

Parks moved to Detroit and in the 1970s, 80s and 90s she continued to press for change in the criminal justice system, in school and housing inequality, in jobs and welfare policy, and in foreign policy. She spoke out against the appointment of Clarence Thomas to the US Supreme Court because she did not approve of his record on civil rights.

When she died at age 92 in 2005, Condoleezza Rice, speaking at her memorial service said that if it had not been for Parks, she probably would never have become Secretary of State.

## Women's Influence through Religion

Three powerful examples of women's religious influence include Catherine Booth, the co-founder of the Salvation Army, Katherine Drexel, heiress, founder of missions schools, and the patron saint of racial justice and philanthropy, and Mary Baker Eddy, founder of The Church of Christ, Scientist. In times when women were not expected to achieve independent accomplishments, each of these women was an independent thinker who forged new paths and made a long-lasting impact on society. Each of their legacies lives on today and continues to grow and evolve.

**Catherine Booth**[96] was born in Victorian England in 1829. She was raised in a Methodist household and read the Bible eight times before age 12. At age 14 she developed spinal curvature and later tuberculosis. She was bedridden for years and spent a great deal of time reading books (becoming assured of her own salvation). When she refused to condemn Methodist reformers in 1850, she was expelled from the church. A year later she met William Booth, who had also been expelled from the Methodists. Since he did not have a church pulpit he took to the streets to preach. They married after a three-year engagement.

In 1859, with her husband's support she wrote a pamphlet, *Female Ministry: Woman's Right to Preach the Gospel,* in defense of Phoebe Palmer, an American preacher. She based her argument that a woman's had a right to preach the gospel on three principles: women were neither naturally nor morally inferior to men; there was no scriptural right to deny women a public ministry; and what the Bible urged, the Holy Spirit had ordained and blessed, and so must be justified. She acknowledged that women fell from grace because of Eve's sin but to leave them there was to reject the good news of the Gospel, which proclaimed that the grace of Christ had restored what sin had taken away and now all men and women were one in Christ.

She spoke about this in public at a time when it was unheard of for women to speak in adult meetings. In 1860 when she began to preach, many Christians were outraged, but after hearing her preach, her husband supported her and became her preaching partner. The Booths began The Christian Mission together in 1865 to help the poor, homeless, and destitute throughout London who were not willing to attend or welcome to join a traditional church. Thieves, prostitutes, gamblers, and drunkards were among their first converts. William Booth spoke to the poor and Catherine Booth spoke to the wealthy to obtain funding. She raised eight children while preaching. In 1874 The Christian Mission had 1,000 volunteers and 42 evangelists. While reading a printer's proof of the 1878 annual report, Booth noticed the statement, "The Christian Mission is a volunteer army." He crossed out the words "volunteer" and wrote in "Salvation Army." Between 1881 and 1885, 250,000 people were converted into The Salvation Army. Catherine became known as the "Army Mother."

The Church of England was hostile to the Salvation Army. However, in 1882 on one weeknight there were almost 17,000 worshipping with the Salvation Army, compared to 11,000 in ordinary churches. Catherine Booth organized Food-for-the-Million Shops where the poor could buy hot soup and a three-course dinner for a sixpence. On Christmas Day and other special occasions, she would cook over 300 dinners to be distributed to London's poor.

Catherine Booth was a political activist. When she found that women and children worked long hours for lower pay than men, she attempted to shame the employers into raising the rates of the women and children and to improve their working conditions. She led a campaign against the way matches were made. Women were paid little, worked 16 hours a day and risked their health when they dipped match heads in yellow phosphorus. The toxic fumes turned the face green and then black, discharging foul smelling pus and eventually causing death. Her campaign argued that harmless red phosphorous be used instead. She died of cancer at age 62 and her husband continued the crusade. By 1901 the use of yellow phosphorous in matchmaking was discontinued.

In an era in which women had few rights, no role in the professional sphere and a minimal presence in church leadership, Catherine Booth was a preacher, an evangelist, a theologian, and co-founder of a religious organization which still thrives. Today it is international, in 130 countries with over 1,500,000 members. In the United States alone The Salvation Army assists approximately 23 million people each year, providing disaster relief, life skills to escape poverty, drug and alcohol rehabilitation, homeless shelters, food pantries, LGBTQ support, summer camps, solutions to human trafficking, job services, veterans' services, services for the aging, help during the holidays, help for domestic abuse, after school programs, and spiritual counseling.

**Katharine Drexel**[97] was born in 1858 in Philadelphia, the daughter of a wealthy American financier and philanthropist. While growing up she watched her father pray for 30 minutes every night. Three times a week her stepmother opened the house and distributed food, clothing, and rent assistance to those in need but too proud to ask for help. Hers was a family that understood the responsibilities that come with great wealth.

A book, *A Century of Dishonor*, by Helen Hunt Jackson addressing the plight of Native Americans inspired her to help and she began a lifelong legacy of personal and financial support of United States missions.

When Drexel's father died in 1865, she and her sisters received the income from a trust fund which in today's dollars would be approximately $400,000,000. The sisters contributed money to help the St. Francis Mission on the Rosebud Reservation in South Dakota. In 1887 the sisters met with Pope Leo XIII to ask for assistance in finding missionaries who would staff some of the Indian missions they had been financing. At that meeting the Pope suggested that Katherine become a missionary herself. She consulted with Philadelphia Bishop James O'Connor because she did not think she was virtuous enough. "I know the privations, the trials, the temptations, and I ask myself, could I go through all these things in a manner suitable for edifying the religious of my order?"

Bishop O'Connor responded, "I was never so sure of any vocation, not even my own as I am of yours." She entered the Sisters of Mercy Convent in 1889. This was not without controversy. Her uncle, Anthony Drexel, tried to talk her out of it. The Philadelphia Public Ledger ran a headline, "Miss Drexel Enters a Catholic Convent - Gives Up Seven Million."

She changed her name to Mother Katharine and along with 13 other women started a religious congregation, The Sisters of the Blessed Sacrament. Three years later they opened their first boarding school, St. Catherine's Indian School in Santa Fe, New Mexico. She asked the Friars in Cincinnati to staff a mission among the Navajos in Arizona and New Mexico on land she had purchased. In 1910 she financed the printing of 500 copies of *A Navaho-English Catechism of Christian Doctrine for the Use of Navaho Children,* written by the Friars.

In 1915 she founded Xavier University in New Orleans, the first Catholic University in the United States for African Americans.

Drexel died in 1955 at age 96. During Drexel's lifetime she established 145 missions, 50 schools for African Americans and 12 schools for Native Americans. The order she established remains in existence today working with African Americans and Native Americans in 21 states and Haiti. Numerous Catholic parishes, schools, and churches bear her name.

Pope John Paul II beatified Drexel on November 20, 1988 (after finding that a man was miraculously cured of his deafness in 1974 and his family had prayed for her intercession). She was canonized on October 1, 2000.

**Mary Baker**[98] grew up in New Hampshire, the youngest of six children. Her father was religious, and her mother was devout and quiet. While young, she had frequent bouts of sudden illness. In 1862 she became a patient of Phineas Quimby, a mental health healer from Maine. Their interactions made a profound impact on her thinking. A homeopath, Quimby believed in hypnosis and mesmerism.

In 1866 she fell on ice in Lynn, Massachusetts, causing a significant spinal injury, and later wrote: "On the third day thereafter, I called for my Bible, and opened it at Matthew, 9:2: *And, behold, they brought to him a man sick of the palsy, lying on a bed; and Jesus seeing their faith said unto the sick of the palsy; Son, be of good cheer; thy sins be forgiven thee.* (King James Bible)]. As I read, the healing truth dawned upon my sense; and the result was that I arose, dressed myself, and ever after was in better health than I had before enjoyed. That short experience included a glimpse of the great fact that I have since tried to make plain to others; namely, Life in and of Spirit: this Life being the sole reality of Existence."

She became convinced that illness could be healed through an awakened thought brought about by a clearer perception of God and the explicit rejection of drugs, hygiene, and medicine, based on her observation that Jesus did not use these methods for healing.

In 1875 she self-published her book, *Science and Health*, later re-titled *Science and Health With Key to the Scriptures*, which she called the textbook of Christian Science. The first print run was 1,000 copies. Initially she taught Christian Science to 800 people. Many of her students also became healers. The last chapter, "Fruitage" contained testimonies of people who claimed to be healed by reading the book. She made numerous revisions to the book during her lifetime.

In 1879 she established the Church of Christ, Scientist, "to commemorate the word and works of our Master [Jesus], which should reinstate primitive Christianity and its lost element of healing."

Her students moved throughout the country, practicing healing, and instructing others. She authorized them to list themselves as Christian Science practitioners. She published a church manual, establishing guidelines that are still followed. In Boston in 1888 she opened a reading room selling Bibles, her writings, and other publications. (This model was replicated and today there are more than 1,000 reading rooms.)

In 1894 the Mother Church was built in Boston and initially she served as its pastor. In 1898 she founded The Christian Science Publishing Society and when she reached the age of 87 she founded *The Christian Science Monitor*, a daily newspaper designed to "injure no man, but to bless all mankind" in response to "yellow" journalism.

Eddy died on December 3, 1910 at age 89. Today it is estimated there are 1,400 Christian Science churches throughout the world and more than 400,000 members world-wide.

In conclusion, power through indirect and direct influence changes society at both local and collective levels.

Each of us has power and when we believe strongly in something on an individual level - whether it be raising a child, teaching a student, mentoring an employee - or something on a much larger scale such as those women who accomplished social reform have, it is possible to focus, harness the power and resources, navigate the obstacles, and make a significant impact.

# Chapter 5:

# Power Strategies

**"The most common way people give up their power is by thinking they don't have any."**

*-Alice Walker*

Female power is strong and unique. Each of us has power. It is innate and part of our nature. Yet not all of us believe that we have it, know whether we want to use it, or understand how we should think about it. Today it is far too easy to feel that it is important for a woman to embrace aspects of masculine power (drive, competition, dominance) and to diminish the aspects of her female power (charm, beauty, collaboration). Denying female power undercuts a woman.

Female power comes from within and begins with the hardwire of nurture, love, empathy, and intuition. As I write these words I can hear friends and colleagues thinking I am wrong, that those words describe the attributes of a female in 1955 and those women had no power; the only way for a woman today to be powerful is to tap into the masculine aspects of power. I can also hear friends and colleagues asking how I could possibly be writing this. In my professional life I have excelled in a field which, when I entered, was still very much male.

I have thought about this long and I hard, I have thought about my professional successes and I have reflected on my successful marriage and my personal life. I know one thing to be fundamentally true: when I feel confident, I have power. When I feel confident, it is not because I am tapping into the masculine aspects of power; it is because I am tapping into my own inner power. When I am confident, I am powerful. When I am powerful, I am effective in what I am setting out to accomplish. I have confidence when I tap into my own innate, instinctual power, understand it, and am not afraid to use it.

It is not enough to understand that I have power. Power on its own is neither good nor bad. A car has power, but if it never leaves the driveway, who cares how much power it has? Power compounds as it is used (and powerlessness compounds as power is not used). It is important to understand how to use power.

Effectively using power requires strategy. Although some use of female power is instinctual, the velocity of the power dramatically increases when strategy is employed. How to use your power strategically in a way that is right for you is a skill that can be learned. Because of the differences between female and male power, strategies to use female power differ from strategies to use male power.

It requires having an open mind and dusting off preconceptions about that 1950's woman and thinking she did not have power. She did have power and the source of that power was not very different from what female (non-masculine) power is today. Strategic use of female power includes the behavioral skills of charm, beauty, and collaboration. What has changed since 1950 is why and where a woman uses these skills. Power strategies one chooses will change and evolve as the circumstances do and as time passes on.

Charm, beauty, and collaboration are strategic behavioral skills that women should embrace.

## Charm

Charm is a strategic power behavioral skill. In an interview with Madeline Albright, Bill Maher commented on the recent string of women occupying global leadership positions and pointedly asked Albright whether she thought women leaders had it easier when negotiating with mostly male foreign leaders because they could flirt in a way that male diplomats simply could not without calling their sexuality into question.[99]

Albright laughed and conceded she used her feminine charm in bilateral negotiations with foreign heads of state. In a 1996 New York Times article, *Madeleine Albright's Audition*, the author notes Albright has made it in a world dominated by men, because of men. She used her wealth and Georgetown home as meeting places for rich, important, and potentially important Democrats. Albright moved up because she worked hard for men, made them look good, and believed in them. ''I was the world's perfect staffer,'' she says, "or the ultimate good daughter."[100]

As defined by Joseph S. Nye, Jr., the former Dean of Harvard's Kennedy School of Government, *soft power* is the ability to influence or lead through persuasion or attraction, by co-opting people rather than coercing them. Soft power is not the exclusive preserve of women (Barack Obama has soft power). However women are more inclined than men to use soft power through tools such as dialogue and engagement rather than the threat of arms or exclusion.[101]

A 2016 Korn Ferry Hay Group Study measured social skills via the Emotional and Social Competency Inventory (ESCI), which tests emotional intelligence. The ESCI tool measures 12 emotional and social intelligence competencies proven to impact business performance: achievement orientation, adaptability, coaching and mentoring, conflict management, empathy, emotional self-awareness, inspirational leadership, influence, organizational awareness, positive outlook, teamwork, and emotional control. The study found women outperformed men in all the categories except "emotional self-control," where no difference was found. The study concludes that all the skills in which the women outperformed the men are essential for successful collaboration with others and indicate why women excel at collaboration.[102]

Professor Yanna J. Weisberg, and her team published the results of a study which found women consistently scored higher than men on agreeableness. Agreeableness comprises traits relating to altruism, such as empathy and kindness. Agreeableness involves the tendency toward cooperation, maintenance of social harmony, and consideration of the concerns of others (as opposed to exploitation or victimization of others). Women also scored higher in Compassion and Politeness. Politeness describes the tendency to show respect to others and refrain from taking advantage of them and is related to traits such as cooperation and compliance. The study finding that women score higher than men on both aspects is consistent with prior research showing women are more trusting and compliant than men.[103]

Charm has power and influence. In 1981 Prince Charles told Ronald Reagan that Nancy Reagan's charm made him a "devoted" admirer for life.[104]

Victoria Pynchon, an attorney and co-founder of *She Negotiates* said that as a litigator her job was to win every skirmish in the long war of attrition that is litigation. "There was no reward for looking good, only being good. And it did not take me long to realize that I could be good using their low opinion of my abilities as my own secret weapon of attack. When I needed their favor, I did not hesitate to use 'feminine charms' to gain it. Those 'charms' included warmth, flattery, playfulness, and sexiness. Bringing them into the field in play in no way diminished my intelligence, savvy, meticulous preparation, and reputation as a worthy adversary."[105]

The stage on which we women are instructed to play, fingers waggling in our faces, is often so constricting it is a wonder we can move at all. To deny ourselves access to any of our powers too often leaves us without any power at all. When I mentor women, I urge them to use whatever they have got. If warmth, playfulness, and flattery get the job done and they are comfortable expressing themselves in these dimensions, by all means, I counsel, go ahead, and use them.

When women paper over that which makes us most human, dimensional, and flexible, we deprive ourselves of what is truly generative within and among us. If we instead attune ourselves to those we want to influence, a well-placed bit of flattery can take us places no amount of earnest argument ever will. If we are true to ourselves and trustworthy players in the business of commerce, our success will be earned fairly and our behavior above reproach.

Flirting works. English writer, Hanna Betts, writes, "Readers, I have a dark confession: I live to flirt. Not flagrant, purposeful, succumb to me now flirtation (though this has its place), but trying to be pleasant, smoothing things over, making the world-go-round type of stuff. Thus far for this week, I have flirted with Swiss train guards, a posse of shy schoolgirls, a Gallic chef, two salesmen, one of my closest friends and an airline pilot. None of this had anything to do with eroticism. Rather it was an attempt to charm the poor blighters - by which I also mean charm something out of them."[106]

Betts notes that women should not be embarrassed that strategic flirtation is largely a female preserve. One can be a feminist and a flirt. Long before the dawning of the feminist era charm had the status of an ancient weapon. Helen of Troy, Eleanor of Aquitaine, and Queen Elizabeth I all used flirtation to flourish.

A 2012 British survey poll of 2,000 commissioned by the website Confused.com,[107] which wanted to investigate gender bias and positive discrimination, found that more than half of British women admitted to flirting with men to get their way, with a fifth saying they did so at work. Survey comments noted that women turned to their feminine wiles to help themselves get ahead, when the situation called for it. It seemed that many women were not afraid to turn to gender at some point or another as a means of benefit, whether it be to flirt their way out of trouble or bag a promotion.

Academic studies back up the power of charm and flirtation. In 2012 Laura Kray, PhD, Professor at the Haas School of Business at the University of California, and her colleagues defined feminine charm as an impressive management technique available to women that combined friendliness with flirtation.[108]

Kray's research found women were confronted with a tradeoff between being perceived as strong or as warm. Using feminine charm in negotiation was a technique that combined both. The aim of feminine charm was to make a partner in an interaction feel good to gain compliance toward broader goals. Flirtation did not mean overt sexual advances. Rather flirtation signaled attractive qualities like confidence, essential to successful negotiators, and socially desirable characteristics like playfulness, flattery, and sexiness. The study found that women who used more social charm were rated as more effective than their partners, in part because flirtation combined with friendliness would flatter and ultimately disarm a negotiating partner. Kray stated that many of her students were senior women executives who admitted they loved to flirt. She maintained flirting was not unprofessional if it remained playful and friendly. The key was to flirt with your own natural personality in mind. Be authentic. Have fun. That would translate into confidence, a strong predictor of negotiation success.

Kray's research examined feminine charm in four separate studies and concluded that the use of feminine charm resulted in female negotiators being perceived as more effective and having greater understanding of their negotiating partner's interests and thus enhanced the positive mood of their interaction partner. The study suggested charm guidelines. Be animated in your body movements. Make frequent eye contact. Smile and laugh (Ditch the poker face). Be playful and give compliments in as sincere a fashion as is possible. ("You're even more charming in person than over email.")

Kray's research also found that because feminine charm combined friendliness with flirtation, its effect appeared to reside in how those two dimensions were balanced. The study showed that when perceived as being flirtatious, female negotiators received better offers than when being perceived as merely friendly.

That is consistent with a study by Fiske which found that warmth alone signaled a lack of intent to pursue self-interest or competitive goals, making friendliness an economic liability in a competitive zero-sum negotiation. Although in some cases friendliness might facilitate the expansion of the negotiating pie and create positive impressions of a female negotiator, the result could become unfavorable if she is perceived as "too nice."

Kray's research also showed that emphasizing warmth alone backfired because it reinforced age-old stereotypes that women were not competitive. Feminine charm, however, allowed females to meet this expectation in a face-to-face competitive context and was a unique female technique for managing negotiator impressions, increasing the proverbial negotiating pie, and, depending on its balance of friendliness and flirtatiousness, determining how resources were divided between the sexes. Kray also notes that charm works best in situations where two parties have a competing interest. Those types of scenarios involve both a concern for oneself (a competitive motive) and a concern for one's negotiating counterpart (a cooperative motive). Kray's study shows that feminine charm helps balance these motives to reach mutually beneficial trade-offs, to create and maintain positive relationships.

Mary Robinson, the first female President of Ireland, a former lawyer and former nun, used her "moral authority" to rally public opinion. When asked if women lead and manage differently than men, she answered, "Obviously it is not black and white, but I do think women tend to be more problem solvers and lead in a more participatory way. It's less hierarchical; there is more listening and nurturing. Everybody gets a chance to say their piece. But when I was elected, I made it very clear that I was going to do the job as a woman. As a nonexecutive president I had to use symbols and the right language to reach out into small communities and the inner city and different parishes and use examples of what was happening there to influence others. So a lot of it was playing to the qualities I feel women have perhaps more strongly.[109]

Pandemics often create communication crises, because leaders must persuade entire populations to suspend their lives due to an invisible threat. The New York Times describes New Zealand's Prime Minister, Jacinda Ardern's Facebook communications as a lesson in rhetorical blending: epidemiology brightened with empathy, law leavened with Mom jokes. And her approach has been strikingly effective. Ardern coaxed New Zealanders ("our team of five million") to buy a lockdown so severe that even retrieving a cricket ball from a neighbor's yard was banned. In some quarters she is called a saint.[110]

A comedian imitating her says she is so nice that "to make fun of Jacinda almost feels like making fun of a puppy." Her politics are known in New Zealand as the politics of kindness, and they have been highly successful.

Susan Spencer, only woman to serve as general manager for an NFL team, argues that if women want to get ahead in business, they need to embrace their femininity, not repress it. She says those women who try to survive by being one of the guys will fail. She thrived by embracing her femininity and feels "feminine charm" got her out of a lot of sticky situations.[111]

As an example, she points to her negotiation with the chair of a Polish company she was trying to convince to move to Michigan. He spoke no English, so they used a translator. She had to use a lot of body language to convey the kind of person and businessperson she was. She made sure to smile, make eye contact, keep her head up and engage him in an animated way. She won him over. She stresses that going overboard flaunting feminine charm can backfire, however, and says an advantage she uses is to team up with another woman. They play any unwanted attention off against the other and often the two women are just too much of a good thing for the guy and he turns to putty in their hands.

Using feminine charm and wiles to gain advantage is not new. As Keith Rinehart explains in *"Shakespeare's Cleopatra and England's Elizabeth,"* the two women were similar in temperament and technique. Both used feminine wiles to gain political advantage. Both were consummate actresses. Both could show the woman behind or within the queen. It was this skill that made them endlessly fascinating. Both women used their innate feminine power for political gain, and this was unusual in their time periods. Queen Elizabeth presented herself as beautiful, desirable, and unattainable which allowed her to play the "marriage game" indefinitely but never actually marry. Cleopatra did much of the same to capture the hearts of Julius Caesar and Mark Antony, both of whom she needed to protect Egypt from Rome's imperialism.[112]

In sum, charm is a powerful behavioral strategy for women to embrace in life and in business. There is more strength in embracing femininity than in repressing it. When using power, one must be cognizant of the context in which it is being used.

## Beauty:

**She Walks in Beauty**

**by** George Gordon, Lord Byron

*She walks in beauty, like the night*
*Of cloudless climes and starry skies.*
*And all that's best of dark and bright*
*Meet in her aspect and her eyes:*
*Thus mellow'd to that tender light*
*Which heaven to gaudy day denies.*

*One shade the more, one ray the less,*
*Had half impair'd the nameless grace*
*Which waves in every raven tress,*
*Or softly lightens o'er her face;*
*Where thoughts serenely sweet express*
*How pure, how dear their dwelling place.*

*And on that check, and o'er that brow,*
*So soft, so calm, so eloquent,*
*The smiles that win, the tints that glow,*
*But tell of days in goodness spent,*
*A mind at peace with all below,*
*A heart whose love is innocent!*

Beauty is powerful. I know when I feel beautiful I feel confident. With confidence comes power. I am sure I am not the only woman who understands that. Every one of us has innate beauty. Strategically thinking about how to improve beauty enhances confidence. Enhancing beauty is a skill. The power of beauty starts from within. Strategically improving it takes work and effort.

As Caroline Kennedy notes[113] Shakespeare's description of Cleopatra is one of the most extravagant in all literature. He makes an explicit connection between beauty and power, describing the elaborate pageantry of Cleopatra's golden barge, her breathtaking loveliness, and the royal authority of her seductive voice. At a time when kings and pharaohs were believed to have divine attributes, and women were powerless and almost nonexistent in the historical record, Cleopatra was truly a wonder of the world.

The feminine beauty ideal changes over the generations and across cultures. The ideal of beauty at the time impacts how a woman views herself. Victorian women were body conscious, tightening corsets to reduce their waistlines and wearing bustles that magnified their buttocks. Women in the 1920s bobbed their hair, wore bold makeup, and hid their curves.

One of the most powerful women in the beauty industry was Estee Lauder. Harvard Business School Professor Nancy Koehn writes that Lauder understood that a trip to the beauty parlor or buying a new lipstick was more than an exercise in the latest fashions. It was also a means for a woman to assert self-confidence at a moment when her family's economic opportunities seemed limited. In the 1930s post-depression period Lauder is quoted as saying, "There was business in beauty as long as there was a woman alive. We have to eat 365 days a year. We get dressed every day. Women take care of their faces with the same consistency. Business is always there if one looks for it. A woman in those hard times would first feed her children, then her husband, but she would skip her own lunch to buy a fine face cream."[114]

Koehn points out that in the 1940s the role of the cosmetic industry was debated. The novelist Fannie Hurst, in a 1942 New York Times Magazine article, *Glamour as Usual?* regarded the pursuit of beauty in the midst of a global conflict as frivolous and wrote, "The history of women's role in this desperate struggle for the free and good way of life will not be written in lipstick."

Others disagreed and in a Letter to the Editor, responding to Hurst, Mrs. Horace L. Harrison, stated the beauty shop or whatever it is which contributes to one's well-being offers a service to humanity. The woman who gets a lift from a new hairdo may just be the one who makes a commendable contribution in any great crisis. She wrote, "Taking care with one's appearance demonstrated women's patriotism. Would we help the brave men fighting for our country if we appear before them tear stained and worn? No, let's lift our heads and send them off with iron in our hearts, a smile on our red lips and a bloom in our cheeks."[115]

In 1943 Maison G. deNavarre wrote that cosmetics have been with mankind since the beginning of time and have withstood every social, political, and religious change in history. During the war years, working women purchased beauty products and paid more attention to their appearance to define their public identities, assert their independence, enjoy themselves, and spend some of the money they were making.[116]

Harvard Business School Professor Richard Tedlow, quotes Revson stating that female wage earners have the ability to indulge themselves in beauty products their rich friends buy[117]. Nancy Koehn posits that perhaps some working women used makeup to maintain their femininity as they took up jobs that historically belonged to men. Postwar Lauder believed women would use consumption to express themselves. In the late 1940s she was pretty sure female consumers wanted beauty offerings that made them feel feminine, sophisticated, and elegant. She was also fairly certain women from a variety of social classes could and would pay premium prices for these products - but only if the advantages that buyers expected to receive from these offerings were equal to or greater than the price premium. She put emphasis on the packaging and on the distribution channels.

In the 1950s Marilyn Monroe and her hourglass figure was perceived as the epitome of beauty. In the 1960s and 1970s Twiggy, Farrah Fawcett and Cher epitomized a thin beauty. In the 1980s Jane Fonda's work-out and aerobics became popular and health became part of beauty.

In 2016 Dove launched its largest ever study to understand women and girls. The Dove Global Beauty and Confidence Report interviewed 10,500 females across 13 countries and found that woman's confidence in their bodies was on a steady decline, with low body esteem becoming a unifying challenge shared by women and girls around the world, regardless of age or geography. This was Dove's third report, building on its 2004 and 2010 studies. It revealed the impact low body esteem had on a woman's ability to realize her potential, with nearly all women (85%) and girls (79%) saying they opted out of important activities, such as trying out for a team or club, and engaging with family or loved ones, when they did not feel good about the way they looked.[118]

In the recent Dove report 7 in 10 girls with low body esteem said they would not be assertive in their opinion or stick to their decision if they were not happy with the way that they looked. Women (69%) and girls (65%) cited increasing pressures from advertising and media to reach an unrealistic standard of beauty as a key force in driving appearance anxiety, while 56% of all women recognized the impact of an "always on" social media culture in driving the pressure for perfection. Nearly eight in ten (78%) of both women and girls felt some pressure to never make mistakes or show weakness.

The Dove report is interesting in that it uncovered a unique tension, with 60% of women believing they need to meet certain beauty standards, while at the same time 77% agreeing it is important to be their own person and not copy anyone else. The majority of women (83%) and girls (77%) said they want to look their personal best rather than follow someone else's definition of "beautiful" and 83% of all women and 82% of all girls agree that every woman has something about her that is beautiful. For many women and girls, the Dove study found that the key to breaking a cycle of beauty and appearance anxiety seems to be the experience of taking time to care for their minds, body, and appearance. Seven in ten women and eight in ten girls reported feeling more confident or positive when they invested time in caring for themselves. Taking time for care -whether it is body or mind - is an important step in improving the confidence of women and girls.

As Caroline Kennedy notes in her book, as girls and young women, we all go through many phases, depending on how we feel about ourselves and our bodies. We try to dress like people we admire - the most popular girls in the class, or celebrities of the moment. It takes time to figure out our own conception of beauty - both outer and inner - and often we return to the images of beauty we formed in our youth, transformed through our lifetime of experience. She notes that while thinking of her grandmothers she now understands it was their faith, bravery, curiosity, and humor, as well as their fashionable hats, that made them beautiful. She also notes that women have a complicated relationship with beauty. The way we present ourselves to the world, our changing sense of self, the pleasure of feeling pretty, the pain of feeling self-conscious, and the freedom that comes with accepting yourself are all important parts of being a woman.

In a 2011 Harvard Business Review opinion piece on gender, executive coach Gill Corkindale notes that sociologist Catherine Hakim shattered the last great taboo of the workplace by saying that professional women should use their "erotic capital"- beauty, sex appeal, charm, dress sense, liveliness, and fitness - to get ahead at work. And rather than believing old notions have only a trivial, superficial value, women should change the way they use the "beauty premium" and not be ashamed of using it to get ahead.[119]

Hakim argues that while we have no problem exploiting our other advantages – money (economic capital), intelligence and education (human capital), and contacts (social capital) - women especially still shirk from using erotic capital. She insists the "beauty premium" is an important economic factor in our careers, citing a US survey that found good-looking lawyers earned between 10 and 12 percent more than dowdier colleagues. She also contends an attractive person is more likely to land a job in the first place and then be promoted.

In a London newspaper Hakim wrote, "Meritocracies are supposed to champion intelligence, qualifications, and experience. But physical and social attractiveness delivers substantial benefits in all social interaction, making a person more persuasive, able to secure the cooperation of colleagues, attract customers, and sell products." She argues that the financial returns of attractiveness now equal the returns of qualifications, with many young women now believing that beauty is as important as education. She uses Christiane Lagarde, the first woman to serve as France's Finance Minister, as the Managing Director of the International Monetary Fund, and as President of the European Central Bank, as a woman who exploits her intelligence, qualifications, and erotic capital.

Executive coach Gill Corkindale shares that her experience is more complex, and that the beauty premium is culturally specific: what works in one country, company, or culture does not always transfer to another. However, she thinks the basic premise is right: if people invest in education, training, qualifications, and work experience, why can they not also invest in themselves?

External beauty is easy to quantify and criticize. In the ZOOM world of the corona virus quarantine, in the era of selfies, Facebook, and social media, presenting yourself visually (and in the case of ZOOM, looking at yourself while you do so) forces a constant evaluation of physical beauty. In this increasingly transparent world it is not just that others are looking at you, but perhaps an even bigger impact on confidence (or lack thereof) is that you are constantly looking at yourself and frequently looking at yourself in comparison to peers who may look better, prettier, more pulled together, more confident, and more powerful.

Research done by psychologist Elaine Hatfield revealed that people tend to assume that attractive people are warm, sensitive, kind, interesting, poised, and outgoing.[120]

Author Emily Armstrong wholeheartedly agreed with the burlesque performer and fan who said that "sexy is a set of skills," and to extend it to "pretty, too, is a set of skills." She is of the opinion that pretty is not about genetic makeup. Pretty is about what she does with her genetic makeup. The skills she uses include makeup, hair styling, fashion, and posture – all of which can be learned and improved by watching YouTube tutorials. Pretty is like good design. It is a set of skills. "You may be attracted by the aesthetic, but, like wandering through Target and picking up beautiful kitchen gadgets of whose function you're wholly unaware, it is important to remember that such artifice holds no intrinsic relationship to the value of the person, or the gadget, it adorns."[121]

For many a woman (even before the ZOOM era), how her hair looks is an important factor in her beauty and confidence. The phrase, "I am having a bad hair day" means more than hair. It means she does not feel attractive. That affects her confidence and her power.

Professor Ingrid Banks notes that hair is one of the first attributes to catch our eye, not only because it is associated with perceptions of attractiveness or unattractiveness, but because hair serves as a badge carrying important political, cultural, and social meanings, particularly in relation to group identity. She notes that hair is one of the most, if not the most significant, topics of discussion among black women.[122]

Willie Morrow notes *in 400 Years Without a Comb* that curly and kinky hair was glorified in West African societies as point of pride and elegance, yet it became a symbol of racial inferiority once enslaved Africans reached the American shores.[123]

Banks notes that by the early part of the twentieth century, African Americans began associating hairstyles with their ability to achieve economic success in a segregated society.

Psychiatrists William H. Grier and Price M. Cobbs focus on the issue of "achieving womanhood" for African American women and argue that the process of grooming hair to assimilate to white dominant standards is not only painful for black girls, but the end result is that the black female children simply look acceptable rather than beautiful, where even if white women endure pain while grooming their hair, the result is that their beauty is enhanced – a beauty that is celebrated even before they enter the salon.[124]

Banks interviewed black women and asked if hair was associated with power in any way. Some interviewees responded that black women who choose to wear their hair natural are participating in a revolutionary act by going against the grain and challenging white standards of beauty. One interviewee responded that "your hair is your crown." Banks notes that "crown" suggests a source of power, excellence, or beauty. Glory is defined as something that makes a person honored or illustrious. Glory also relates to pride and pride to self-esteem. Pride suggests a high or inordinate opinion of one's importance as displayed through one's conduct, physical appearance, or in some other way. Therefore, a notion of power is embedded in the idea of hair as a black woman's crowning glory. Hair can become a foundation for understanding how black women view power and its relationship to self-esteem. Other interviewees discussed power as it relates to having personal choice and autonomy in hairstyling decisions. One argued it takes a strong woman to exercise the choice to wear her hair naturally as it goes against mainstream standards of femininity.

Professor Blain Roberts shows the role of female beauty in the economic empowerment of black women. During the depression black beauty salons and barber shops became important in the lives of working-class African Americans in the southern United States. The beauty process also provided overworked black women opportunities for relaxation and pampering. Black women could enter the profession with little capital. In the first two decades of the twentieth century dozens of black women went into business for themselves, selling hair pomades and hair growers (shampoo), door to door and through mail order.[125]

The two most famous, Annie Turbo Malone and Madame C.J. Walker shared their hair care systems with thousands of southern black women. Both suffered from diseased scalps and brittle hair and took advantage of the fact that barriers to entering the hair care product market were low. They experimented in their homes and created systems of hair care regime. Madam Walker emphasized the maintenance of a healthy, well-groomed body as key to the cultivation of personal and racial pride, and as an antidote to the negative image of black women that was pervasive during that day. They became official agents for their companies and reaped the profits from door to door sales, from their own company-affiliated beauty shops, and from women they recruited as agents. With their system black women were able to support their families.

At the Thirteenth Annual Convention of the National Negro Business League in 1912, Walker told the audience of her spectacular financial success and offered her annual revenues for the past seven years as evidence. Beauty culture provided her a way out of the low paying menial jobs most black women were forced to take. She said, "I am a woman that came from the cotton fields of the South; I was promoted from there to the wash-tub; then I was promoted to the cook kitchen, and from there I promoted myself into the business of manufacturing hair goods and preparations. Everybody told me I was making a mistake by going into this business, but I know how to grow hair as I know how to grow cotton."[126]

In the early 1920s Walker and Malone added skincare cosmetics including face powders. This was a significant move in that hairdressing had its roots in black culture; doing make-up did not. Malone and Walker did not manufacture skin bleaching or lightening agents. Some black women insisted that cosmetics gave them an edge in "the game of life" as one Georgia woman wrote in a beauty column sponsored by the Lariuse Beauty Foundation, a St. Louis cosmetics company. 1920 ads from the Walker company emphasized that "no greater force is working to glorify the womanhood of our race than Walker hair and skin preparations." The success of Walker's work was two-fold: 1) it empowered black women to own their own businesses, control their own income and support their families and 2) it developed the beauty culture where women could enjoy welcome moments of pampering, self-indulgence, and sociability.

Embedded in the practice of the beauty culture were moments of physical pleasure and emotional connection. Madame Walker believed that helping clients relax during their appointments was just as important as helping them look better. As a former sharecropper and laundress, she understood that the ritual of shampooing and styling might represent the only occasion a working woman had to unwind. Beauticians provided patrons a physical attractiveness that directly challenged views of black women as degraded and subhuman. Leaving the beauty shop with the knowledge that one's appearance would strike observers as stylish or pretty was a potentially uplifting and empowering experience.

For feminists, beauty can be a dilemma. Professors Sarah Riley and Christina Scharff in their cooperative inquiry study, *Feminism v. Femininity? Exploring Feminist Dilemmas Through Cooperative Inquiry Research*,[127] explored the tensions participants experienced in negotiating their feminist identification on the one hand and their beauty practices on the other. The participants associated beauty practices with regulatory and normative forms of femininity, understanding that feminism critiques feminine beauty practices.

This led to talk of "betraying" feminism, labelling themselves as "bad feminists" or questioning how other feminists might judge them. This created a "dilemma of beauty" in which participation in normative female beauty practices produced both feelings of pleasure and shame. Participants in the study made sense of their engagement with beauty practices in two ways: (1) They either made individualist arguments ("I'm doing it for me") or (2) they understood their beauty practices as adherence to a set of cultural beauty norms of which they were critical. The research supported the point of view that taking up second wave feminist critiques of consumer-oriented beauty ideals while still participating or enjoying them led women to feel they were not good enough or effective enough feminists.

That is interesting because many beauty practices are often made sense of through discourses on autonomy, choice, and pleasure (L'Oréal's slogan, "Because I am worth it"). The root of these discourses could be feminism.

There is a third wave of feminism that reworks traditional associations of femininity with beauty and sexual attractiveness. For "Girlie girls," femininity is not opposed to feminism, but is positioned as central to politics of agency, confidence, and resistance. Contemporary young women have the confidence and position in the world to enjoy "girlie" practices in a way that second-wave feminists did not. Drawing on the "feminism versus feminist" dilemma, Baumgardner and Richards in their book accuse second-wave feminists of making young women feel fraudulent for not being "real" feminists because of their pleasurable participation in consumer-oriented beauty culture.

The feminist feminine dilemma crosses cultures.[128] Journalist Aamna Mohdin writes that black women have a different relationship with femininity than white women. In a recent study on the role of men and women in society, the Pew Research Center asked black women, white women, and Hispanic women, "How Feminine Are You?" 46% of black women were most likely to see themselves as feminine, followed by 42% of Hispanic women and 27% of white women.

American black women were not just more likely to identify as feminine; they were also more likely to embrace it. This was highlighted in a 2007 study that found black women were more interested than their white counterparts in traditionally feminine behaviors such as wearing attractive clothing and also more likely to describe themselves as feminists. For black women, a high level of importance on wearing feminine clothes was a significant positive predictor of feminism, while for white women it was a negative predictor of feminism.

Adia Harvey Wingfield, professor of sociology at Washington State University in St. Louis notes that in a society that has deemed black women incapable of being vulnerable, warm, beautiful, and caring, it can be a powerful choice to identify as feminine. In contrast Wingfield notes white women have historically been the default when it comes to mainstream, cultural ideas of what femininity is and what it looks like. White women do not have to assert or even think a lot about being defined or seen as feminine.[129]

Lauren Fannin, a Professor at Georgia State University who researches the intersection of race, gender and class, notes that while black women embrace femininity to overcome a dehumanization that can be traced back to slavery in the US, white woman's disavowal of femininity is rooted in second wave feminism, which sprang up in the 1960s and focused on challenging gender roles in the family and workplace as well as reproductive rights. Fannin further notes that as a result, the way we understand femininity between black and white women is similar, but the ways in which we respond to it and embrace it is different.[130]

Each of us has a unique beauty. How we think about beauty changes as we pass through the aging phases of life. The power of beauty is a behavioral skill that each of us must consistently work on in this rapidly changing world. It is interesting in a world with cameras that show every flaw in photos, on TV, the movies, and on every Zoom call, we are all forced to look at ourselves and others under microscopes that did not exist in the 1920s or 1930s. Avoiding beauty is no longer an option. Understanding our beauty and working with our beauty is an option we should choose. When we pay attention to our own beauty, we gain confidence. Confidence is power and we should choose it.

## Collaboration:

For centuries women have understood the innate power of collaboration. It is instinctive for women to gather and collaborate. The sewing circle and today's giving clubs form strong bonds and connections. The connection of women to women matters to women. Collaboration among women is powerful and impactful. When women connect with one another and share their strengths, it increases everyone's well-being.

Anne Devereaux-Mills, founder of Parlay House,[131] a collection of discussion salons, believes there is a direct correlation between connection and happiness. She surveyed women and found that receiving a kind action was so powerful that many replicated it themselves. It made the women feel capable of contributing to each other's lives in a meaningful way and that set off a chain reaction: by using what comes easily to you, you disproportionately help someone else struggling in that area, and that feels fabulous. Then that woman figures out what her strengths are and does that for someone else.

She encourages women to find their superpower, saying that most discount their strengths and focus on what they do not do well. Building up a woman's support network starts with empathy because when we stop judging and putting ourselves in the shoes of other people it will allow us to be supportive rather than look for weaknesses. Parlay wants what she calls "four quarters instead of 100 pennies" - a few deep and meaningful relationships with people for whom she could be there and who would be there for her - and not with people who would leave when the going gets tough. Instead she stresses that by truly seeing one another with our wonderful imperfections and individual needs, we are likely to be stronger when we combine forces than when we tear others down.[132]

Are women better off to collaborate in the workforce today? There are certainly pluses and minuses to that in this complicated world. In today's business world, "A woman alone has power; collectively we have impact." In forming the Girls Lounge the founder, Shelley Zalis, discovered two things: there is power in the pack and you realize your strengths make the table better.[133]

Collaboration can help advance careers. Research in the Harvard Business Review[134] finds that while both men and women benefit from having a network of well-connected peers across different groups, women who also have an inner circle of close female contacts are more likely to land executive positions with greater authority and higher pay, while there was no link found for the success of men in terms of the gender composition of their inner circles. The reason posited for this is that women trying to rise up into leadership face cultural and systemic hurdles that make it harder for them to advance, such as unconscious bias. The study suggests that a way to overcome some of these hurdles is to form close connections with other women, who can share experiences from women who have been there, done that - from how to ask for what you're worth to bringing your unique talents to the table. Women are now building circles of trust and have each other's backs.

Pam Kaufman, President of Viacom/Nickelodeon Global Consumer Products, believes it is important to build a support network of people off whom she can bounce ideas, to whom she can go for advice, and who can pick her up when she needs a boost. A squad of support for each other acts as connectors to people and opportunities.[135]

Research shows women to be more nurturing, team oriented, and collaborative. Collaboration is not one size fits all, however, and is not effective in every situation. "No matter how superb your breaststroke, using it to cross a desert is futile. Being collaborative in the wrong situations is similar."[136]

Dr. Pam Heim, author of several books on gender differences indicates men and women view collaboration differently. Women are more likely to agree with the statement, "Being a good team player means helping all of my colleagues with what they need to get done." Men are more likely to agree with the statement, "Being a good team player is knowing your position and playing it well." She also notes that women are less likely to carve out the time during the workday to focus on their top priorities because they feel guilty or selfish doing that. If women do carve out time, they tend it give it away if someone needs them. Studies indicate this means women often end up overscheduled and this can have negative consequences on their careers because they risk appearing scattered, late, and unprepared. They will not have time for focused work and their contributions may not be noticed if they are fragmented.[137]

A Harvard Business Review piece on "*Collaboration's Hidden Tax on Women's Careers*, makes it clear that collaboration can be a double-edged sword because an overemphasis on consensus can be viewed as weak. They identified that collaboration could go wrong for women for several reasons, including asking for permission, appearing indecisive, and failing to assert a strong point of view. They concluded that being a collaborative leader is a tremendous asset in balance. Women who can retain this core ability while at the same time acting decisively to make things happen will have the skills and demeanour to thrive in the future.

A 2017 global survey of education, "Girls are better than boys a working together to solve problems," tested 125,000 15-year-olds in 52 countries and found that girls were 1.6 more likely than boys to be top performers in collaborative problem solving, while boys were 1.6 times more likely than girls to be low achievers. (It is interesting to note that a prior 2012 individual problem-solving test found that boys performed better than girls when working on their own.)[138]

It seems to me that women do have an instinct to collaborate. I know that I have a very strong group of friends, my "kitchen cabinet" and that "kitchen cabinet" is a different group of women when I am addressing work issues and when I am addressing personal issues. Having a group of women I can talk to openly and honestly is very important to me and has been priceless when I have faced significant challenges. I applied for my first job as a lawyer and never applied for another one because along the way women I knew told me about an opening in a law firm and introduced me to those in charge. Along the way I have also done that for many other women. Networks do matter. Respect for the networks we build and establish through life is a skill. Each year I am amazed at how much of my business derives from the relationships with those I have known for decades and stayed in touch with. Understanding the power of collaboration, when to use it, and the importance of having a network is a skill we must continuously work on. When we harness the collaborative instincts women have and work together, we women will accomplish great things for ourselves, those we love, our community, and society.

## Chapter 6:

# How to Keep Your Power

**"Women need solitude in order to find again the true essence of themselves."**

*— Anne Morrow Lindbergh*

It is important to understand that our own power is a personal, priceless resource that must be maintained and nurtured. If we do not tend our power base, it will dissipate. We keep our internal power base by maintaining economic independence, and by fueling our confidence, energy, and business connections through friendship.

I know my instinct is to first focus on the needs of others, and then myself. I also know that to maintain my internal power source it is important to step back, focus on myself, and reflect. It is important that I have a room at home that it is my own space, that I can write in, read in, journal in, and "lock the door."

It is important to me to walk for a few miles every day alone with no music, sounds or agenda and let the thoughts flow. It is important to me that I spend time at the beginning of each week focusing on my goals and priorities and reflecting on where I am now and what the future holds. It is important to me to listen to classical music while I am working. It is important to me to be organized about my creativity. Often I have three to five projects ready to go, organized in a tote bag and I take the bag to the public library and hide for three or four hours to focus.

My power increases when it is not diluted, when I have stopped doing six things at once, reflected and focused on what is important to me, and said NO to what is distracting from my time and energy.

It is important to me to maintain strong friendships with women I have met through the stages of my life and be able to be open and honest about whatever issues I am facing, hear their thoughts, and be there and listen when one of them wants to talk. It is important to me to retain my inner world. I do not think that I am unusual. Many women have that same instinct of putting others first and must figure out ways to maintain their own internal power source.

## A Room of Her Own.

Virginia Woolf's famous 1929 essay, "A Room of Her Own,"[139] argued literally and figuratively that a woman writer should have a room of her own (with lock and key) and enough money to support herself.

In *Gift from the Sea*,[140] Anne Morrow Lindbergh reflects about maintaining a sense of self and internal power. "I find there is a quality to being alone that is incredibly precious. Life rushes back into the void, richer, more vivid, fuller than before.

"I want first of all... to be at peace with myself. I want a singleness of eye, a purity of intention, a central core to my life that will enable me to carry out these obligations and activities as well as I can. I want, in fact - to borrow from the language of the saints - to live 'in grace' as much of the time as possible. I am not using this term in a strictly theological sense. By *grace* I mean an inner harmony, essentially spiritual, which can be translated into outward harmony. I am seeking perhaps what Socrates asked for in the prayer from the Phaedrus when he said, 'May the outward and inward man be one.' I would like to achieve a state of inner spiritual grace from which I could function and give as I was meant to in the eyes of God.

"Woman must come of age by herself...She must find her true center alone. If one sets aside time for a business appointment, a trip to the hairdresser, a social engagement, or a shopping expedition, that time is accepted as inviolable. But if one says: *I cannot come because that is my hour to be alone*, one is considered rude, egotistical, or strange. What a commentary on our civilization, when being alone is considered suspect; when one has to apologize for it, make excuses, hide the fact that one practices it—like a secret vice!"

Time is a treasure that women do not safeguard to the extent they should. After reading a book[141] on the daily rituals of creative artists, Brigid Schulte pointed out that male creative geniuses of the past were protected by the women in their lives and had time to be creative. Martha Freud laid out Sigmund Freud's clothes every morning and put toothpaste on his toothbrush. Marcel Proust's housekeeper brought him his daily coffee, newspapers and mail on a silver tray and did errands at his beck and call. Karl Marx's wife and children lived in squalor while he spent his days writing at The British Museum. Gustav Mahler married a composer and then forbade her to compose, saying there could be only one in the family. He expected her to keep the house silent for him.[142]

Women creative geniuses, however, did not have that luxury. George Sand always worked late at night because she cared for her grandmother during the day. Alice Munro wrote in the "slivers" of time she could find between housekeeping and childrearing. Maya Angelou checked herself into a hotel room to think, read and write. In an interview Patti Scialfa spoke of how difficult it was for her to write music for her solo album because her children kept interrupting her in a way they would never interrupt their father, Bruce Springsteen.[143]

It is difficult for women to carve out the time they need to be creative. Women still spend much more time than men doing housework and childcare. As Melinda Gates noted, "Indeed I have been trying to carve out time to think and write this essay for more than four months. Every single time I've sat down to start, I've gotten a panicked call or email from my husband, son, or daughter; my mother dealing with the strange frontier and endless paperwork of the newly widowed; a credit card company; or a mechanic about some emergency or other that requires my immediate attention to stave off another disaster."

Extensive interviews with elderly to obtain a "lifetime perspective" on how to maintain mental health indicate that because women shoulder more of the caretaking and household-running duties, many felt they did not have enough time for themselves or felt guilty when they focused on their own needs. Many of the women in the study sought privacy - a "room of one's own" - where they could "avoid constant demands and interruptions. This room of one's own did not necessarily mean a physical space, but rather the right to and possibility of a life of one's own. Forms of privacy included gainful employment, a separate bedroom, and their own social engagements.[144]

There is power in solitude. Plautilla Nelli, was a sixteenth-century self-taught painter and nun. Her masterpiece painting, "Last Supper," made its debut after 450 years in hiding. Nelli ran an all women's artist workshop in her convent. Her status as a nun enabled her to pursue art at a time when women were all but banned from the profession.[145]

Renaissance nunneries "extracted women" from domestic duties such as marriage and motherhood, freeing them to engage in other activities. "We think of these nuns as imprisoned but it was a very enriching experience for them." In the convent Nelli found the privacy and seclusion she needed.[146]

In a world that is getting faster and faster, many women today need to be creative about how to block out enough time for themselves to go to a "room of their own" and recharge. Meditation can be very effective to focus and reduce stress. There are different types of meditation (guided meditation, mantra meditation, mindful meditation, Qi gong and Tai Chi, Transcendental meditation, yoga). You can meditate anywhere and you can find the meditation method that works best for you. Some people meditate by taking a long walk in silence. Some people meditate by sitting in a comfortable place and shutting out the world. Some people meditate with prayer. When you meditate, you clear away distracting thoughts and focus. This can bring a new perspective, increase your self-awareness, and focus on the present. With mindful mediation (which is rooted in Buddhism) you "go with the flow," establish consciousness, observe your flow of inner thoughts, emotions, and bodily sensations, and focus on them without judging any thought as good or bad. It teaches you the skill of coming back to focus when you wander.[147]

Meditation is useful, even if you can only carve out 20 minutes a day. It allows you to step back, focus, and re-group. It is important that each of us turn off the smartphone and shut the door for some period of time each day. We need to build self-reflection and silence into our lives, whether it is through journaling, meditating, or going for long, quiet walks. When we do that, we have the space to recharge.

Travel can provide insights and perspective. Some of the most interesting insights I have had about myself and my life have occurred while traveling to different countries, exploring history, art, and cultures. Ten years ago, while in Venice I was inspired to lock myself in the beautiful study in an elegant hotel each morning for three hours and write a TV pilot, something I did not contemplate doing when I left for Venice and something I had never done before.

In an essay utilizing tourism research to understand what motivates women to travel alone and the impact that has on their lives, Erica Wilson and Candice Harris write that travel - particularly independent forms of travel where control over one's own choices is central - can be empowering. "Meaningful travel involves women searching for an increased sense of self and reconsidering other perspectives of life, society, and their relationships with others."[148]

Independent travel serves as a metaphorical "room of one's own" as it is an opportunity to make your own choices and take responsibility for your own life. It is also an escape from daily duties and the demands of others. Independent travel gives women space for reflection and the chance to prioritize time for their own needs and wants.

The concept of a room of one's own is not unique to America. It is global. In their book, "*Words not Swords*," Iranian-American scholar, Farzaneh Milani and Karla Morton address the issues women in Iran face. They write that a woman not only needs a room of her own, but also the freedom to leave it and return to it at will, for a room without that right becomes a prison cell.[149]

Women's empowerment - defined as a composite measure of gender equality in economic participation and decision making, political participation and decision making, and power over economic resources - is twice as great in free economies as in unfree economies. Where women can control their own finances they are more likely to take an active role in the community.[150]

As Virginia Woolf noted, having economic independence is important to maintaining your sense of self. When you have your own bank account, own charge card, own stash, it allows you to sustain whatever project you are working on – whether it be personal, cosmetic, a shopping trip, an image consultant, a career coach, a day with friends, or a trip to the spa. When you are in control of that stash, you know what you can do when you need to or want to. It is important to have the ability to invest in yourself. There have been several times in my life when spending money to improve something that needed improving mattered. Sometimes you must pay for knowledge, and knowledge is power.

To maintain power having a strong support network and good friends matters.

A 2011 study of 2000 women in China published in the *Journal of Clinical Oncology*, found that breast cancer patients with close social and emotional ties in the first six months after diagnosis had better survival rates and fewer recurrences within the first few years.[151]

Researchers at the Vanderbilt-Ingram Cancer Center and their colleagues at the Shanghai Institute of Preventive Medicine found that women with the highest satisfaction with marriage, family, and friends had a 38% reduced risk of mortality and a 48% lower risk of recurrence when compared with those women with poor social ties. Women who reported "favorable" interpersonal relationships had a 35% lower risk. Dr. Meira Epplien, one of the lead researchers commented that the biggest surprise was that physical well-being was less important than strong social ties in breast cancer outcomes.[152]

Friendships empower in business too. In a study of MBA graduates, Brian Uzzi found that women were more likely to be successful in their careers if they had an "inner circle" of close female contacts.[153]

Uzzi hypothesized that such a network can provide critical private information on job opportunities and challenges - anything from whether a firm has equal advancement opportunities for men and women to what an interviewer may ask and the best way to respond. He suggested that women benefit from a strategic approach to networking by seeking quality over quantity in their overall network. Who you know is more important than how many people you know.

In an interview-based study of domestic friendships, Professor Anne Cronin of University of Lancaster (England) found that mothers' connections with other mothers provide support and help women maintain their power. The participants described how having friends with children and sharing maternal experiences, had a positive impact on the emotions and challenges of motherhood. The data revealed these friendships showed a profound positive effect on the participant's own sense of self.[154]

This is a world in which it is very easy to be distracted. The world is coming at us. At the gym on the treadmill watching the tv, the bottom scroll is distracting me. Everyone wants an immediate answer to an email. All is urgent. There is nothing you can do that does not have a heightened level of distraction and a heightened sense of immediateness.

Our times are changing rapidly. Our world has changed more in the last 100 years than in the previous thousand. We split the atom, probed the psyche, invented plastic, perfected airplanes, and robots, put televisions and computers in most homes and mobile phones in most hands. We have changed the way we interact, travel, communicate, learn, work, organize our communities, create and distribute resources, and affect our planet and, in so doing, we have changed our relationship with time. It is all faster and it seems to require immediate responses.

The times to reflect that were built into lives before (working hard on a farm, focusing on physical labor and allowing the mind to be free, having a "day of rest" Sunday to reflect, and not work) are gone. The impact of the speeding up of time is the reality that we have no time. Unless we are proactive, the lack of time controls us and dissipates our power.

It is important to remember that power is an energy resource that we must work to keep and restore, and that work involves focusing on our strengths, carving out time for ourselves, maintaining some economic independence, and relying on the strength of good friendships.

## Chapter 7:

# Woman's Fear of Power

**"No one can make you feel inferior without your consent."**

*- Eleanor Roosevelt*

Are women threatened by their own innate power? Do women understand they have power? Have they thought about how to use it? Are they afraid of what will happen when they use it? Do women believe if the power is feminine, it is not accepted in today's culture? Do women define power in masculine terms? Do women associate power with negative adjectives, such as egocentric or aggressive? Are women afraid that using power will make them stand out from their pack of colleagues and friends? Do women underutilize their own power? If so, why?

I can think of times personally and professionally when I know that I held power back. I did that because at the time I did not have confidence. No one who meets me now would ever believe it but growing up I was so shy I could not deal with strangers. I could not ask questions in a classroom. I cried when on a Sunday the church was so crowded I had to sit by myself, apart from my family. As a young teenager I fainted in public once to avoid talking to a stranger. I was never picked for a sports team and in high school I was never picked for a dance partner. I lived in fear. It has been a long journey and as I got older, it became more complicated.

A memorable example to me was when, as a young lawyer, I had started a speaking career. To improve my speaking and ability to be hired by clients I hired a speech coach who asked me to start and show him the beginning of my presentation. Three minutes into it, he stopped me and told me I was very confusing. I was providing content and yet flipping my hair (I was in my 20s) as if I were looking for a husband. He was distracted and he was sure the audience would be too. He told me to figure out which I wanted and project the right image.

He was right. I wanted both.

Sometimes the actions are accidental or naïve. Sometimes they come from being young. But they also stem from a lack of confidence and a lack of focus. It took me a long time to understand that "Prince Charming" (be it a husband or a metaphor for a career) would not happen unless I focused and tapped into my own power.

It took me longer to understand that power is a process. Owning, claiming, and connecting to your power is necessary but not sufficient. You must pay attention to how you choose to use your power, and how much of it you want to use. Power is not static. It is both a noun and a verb. You have power and you control how you use it – never, not much, or as much as you are able. Sometimes you may choose to be very powerful. Other times, you may hold back your power.

You control your power by your focus, actions, and words. How and when you choose to use your power is evolutionary.

The more you tap into your power the more you find that the power source does not have a limit. And sometimes you need to kick yourself forward into your power zone.

Years ago, when I was afraid to call someone, a good friend asked me if I felt more confident at home or at the office and that wherever it was, I should go there and make the call. At that time, my answer was my office and I did go there and make that personal call. It was interesting how changing the physical environment affected my use of personal power and confidence.

I have also found that if being powerful in a professional setting is important - if I am negotiating a settlement, if I am dealing with a difficult client - it is important to me to carefully pick out what I am wearing and how my hair and makeup is done. For me, being pulled together physically makes me feel more powerful (and I also subscribe to what a college friend's mother told me a long time ago: when you have pulled yourself together, look in the mirror once and don't look again. Assume you look that way the entire day).

How you dress can also make you appear less powerful. It is tricky. Appearing less powerful sometimes makes you more powerful. I remember watching a woman in a contentious divorce who wanted to appear vulnerable before the judge. She deliberately wore a very feminine, frilly yet modest dress and made sure her demeanor was submissive, looking down and then up when asked a question under cross examination.

How each of us connect to our power is very personal. It starts within and is manifested externally. Being aware of our own power and how it is projected matters.

Mary Catherine Bateson, the linguist and anthropologist (and daughter of Margaret Mead and Gregory Bateson) wrote in her book, "Composing a Life,"[155] that life is an improvisational art at every age. We live with constant change. "I like to think of men and women as artists of their own lives, working with what comes to them through accident or talent to compose and recompose a pattern in time that expresses who they are and what they believe in, making meaning even as they are studying and working and raising children, creating and recreating themselves."

Essentially, as career coach Joan Michelson[156] writes in her Forbes column, women tend to integrate work into a greater life "design" rather than designing their life to fit their work. They "zigzag" more than men do, choosing to take career breaks or to take new jobs rather than follow a consistent trajectory. Women naturally take many different routes in their lives, with a holistic approach.[157]

In a world which is rapidly changing Professor Lauren Carstensen, the Director of the Stanford Center on Longevity,[158] opines it is time to get serious about the redesign of life. Thirty years were added to average life expectancy in the 20$^{th}$ Century and rather than imagining the scores of the ways we could use them to improve the quality of our lives, we tacked them on to the end. Therefore, most people are anxious about the prospect of living for a century or more. She mentions that long lives are not the problem. The problem is living in cultures designed for lives half as long as the ones that we have. The Stanford Center on Longevity launched an initiative, "The New Map of Life," convening a group of experts including engineers, cultural scientists, pediatricians, climate scientists, geriatricians, behavioral scientists, financial experts, biologists, educators, health care providers, human resource consultants, and philanthropists. They were charged with the responsibility of envisioning what vibrant, century-long lives would look like and then begin the remapping process.

They agreed it would be a mistake to replace the old, rigid model of life – education, then family and work, and finally retirement - with a new rigid model. Instead, they concluded there should be many different routes, interweaving leisure, work, education, and family throughout life, taking people from birth to death with places to stop, rest, change course and repeat steps along the way. Old age wouldn't last longer. Rather youth and middle age would. All stages of life need to be rethought. Work must change. Maintaining physical fitness through life will be important. Financing longevity needs new framing.

What I found interesting about the Stanford study is that women are already doing this and have found power in managing their lives in this nonlinear fashion. The choices that women make in composing their lives depend on their goals and objectives at the time. A woman may decide to work first, have children and work part-time and work later, or she may choose to not work at all, or she may choose to have children first, then work. Or she may go back to college at age 50, or start a business when others are retiring.

Thinking that you must live your life in linear fashion undercuts your power. Understanding that the world is catching up with how women have always had to live their lives and accepting it is powerful.

So how do you compose your life? How do you use your power? At home and at work? How do you value your own worth? Does it correspond to how you handle your financial assets? If you are feminine, are you weak? Are you powerful only when you exercise powers typically attributable to men? Can you admit to being female and feminine today and say that it is powerful? Is it too soon for women to feel confident with female power in the workforce? Is it too soon for women who work to be feminine at home and at work? How is power expressed? How is this changing in a post COVID world? The issues are complex and evolving.

For women, one way to determine how much personal power they are utilizing is found in how they deal with financial issues. Barbara Huson (formerly known as Barbara Stanny), the author of "Prince Charming Isn't Coming: How Women Get Smart about Money" and "Secrets of Six Figure Earning Women: Surprising Strategies to Up Your Earnings and Change Your Life," is the daughter of the "R" of H & R Block.[159] She writes that she gave her father, then her husband, her money and wealth to handle. One day when she went to the ATM machine she found that her husband had lost all their investments in illegal deals and left her with an income tax bill of more than one million dollars. Her husband left the country. She asked her father for a loan to pay the taxes. He declined, telling her that it was her problem and she had to figure it out. She had three small children. She sought the help of a financial mentor.

Working with the mentor and writing two groundbreaking books in her search for figuring out the answers, she earned her way out of financial trouble and into financial prosperity. She found that women who wait for "Prince Charming"- a man, an inheritance, someone, or something to financially rescue them - are doing themselves a real disservice because "Prince Charming" is not coming.

A journalist by training, she began to interview women who were high earners from all walks of life and levels of net worth. She discovered they had common characteristics. It turns out the under-earning women had common characteristics too. Under-earning is self-imposed by the woman on the woman. Typical under-earners work hard, yet do not have control of their finances, do not balance their checkbooks, have debt, and are ashamed to admit that money matters to them.

Barbara's interviews also led her to believe that financial success is within reach of every woman who wants it and who embraces wanting it; this is a profit motive. She puts forward practical strategies women can take to stop being under-earners, including financial know how (such as ripping open all the unpaid bills, adding debt up, getting a clear financial picture of where you are now), feeling and addressing fear, understanding that working hard does not mean working all the time, and exhibiting audacity, resilience, self-awareness, and non-attachment.

Over the years I have found that to be true. Again, too many women grow up believing the fairy tale that one day "Prince Charming"- a man, an inheritance, a lottery win, some other external force - will come along and rescue them, the damsels in distress. Believing that Prince Charming is coming on his white horse to sweep you up and rescue you prevents you from taking personal responsibility for achieving your own personal success. My experience is that "Prince Charming" does not have to come in the result of a huge windfall or lottery win. If you become a little more strategic, it can result from your annual compensation and salary review and you must ask for it.

Men know that no one is going to tap them on the shoulder and say, "You have done great work. Here is an unexpected bonus or raise." They know that they must position themselves and ask for it. Women unfortunately are more likely to sit there waiting for that tap on the shoulder.

When I was in high school I wanted a summer internship or a job with *The Boston Globe* and my uncle got me an interview with a man there who was very high up. The interview went well. I was sure he liked me and was therefore shocked when my uncle informed me that I was going to be offered neither an unpaid internship nor the job. Yes, he said, the man had in fact liked me a great deal. He had decided not to offer me a job because I did not ask for a job. I did not ask!

I was shocked. I thought someone who liked me and saw my potential would offer me a position. It never crossed my mind to ask for it. Asking for it is not an instinct women have. I have put a lot of thought into why that is so. It could be fear of failure. Women worry that if they ask it and do not get it, they have failed and not received the "A." It could be that for women asking for something and not getting it is personal rejection.

Men understand the concept of "planned rejection." This is an actual strategy to ask for something you know you will not get - yet. The rejection is planned, and part of the overall strategy is to put the "ask" up front and center in people's minds so the process of asking for it will unfold, and the negotiation will begin. To men, asking for it and not getting it is not personal.

Perhaps women do not ask for it because they think when they ask for it they will appear too aggressive. It could be because underneath it all women expect to be taken care of and think that someone is going to notice their good behavior and just reward them. It could be that women have a hard time asking for it because they care about their relationships with their peers and feel that if they ask for it and end up ahead of others in their peer group they will no longer be accepted, and the peer group is a very comfortable place to be.

Asking for it is a skill and it takes a lot of time and practice to learn it.

And, as it turns out, power and ambition are connected. Deborah Tannen, a linguistics professor, in her ground-breaking article for Harvard Business Review in 1995, "The Power of Talk: Who Gets Heard and Why?" focuses on the words men and women use. Even so small a linguistic strategy as the choice of a pronoun can affect who gets credit. She notes that in her research she hears men say "I" in situations where women say "we." As an example, a male publishing executive said, "I'm hiring a new manager. I'm going to put him in charge of my marketing division," as if he owned the corporation. In stark contrast the women said, "we" when referring to work they alone had done. One woman explained it would be too self-promoting to claim credit in an obvious way by saying "I did this." Yet she expected - sometimes in vain - that others would know it was her work and would give her the credit she did not claim for herself.

Studies show that women are more likely to downplay their certainty and men are more likely to minimize their doubts. It is interesting because the impression that comes across as a lack of confidence may not actually be a lack of confidence. It may just be the desire not to appear boastful.

Attorney Lauren Stiller Rikleen notes that throughout her career as a lawyer and consultant she has seen hundreds of successful women whose careers stalled at levels that did not match their ambitions for themselves. These women were not held back by work ethics or skills. And they were not held back by family pressures. They admitted they faced unconscious bias at the office, but they did not see that as insurmountable. Instead she contends that discomfort with mastering what Stanford Professor Jeffery Pfeiffer[160] calls "power dynamics" is the problem. Women are far more likely to view their workplace as a meritocracy where good work will be rewarded, and men are much more aware of the role influence and power play in getting ahead.[161]

A strong first step must be to become more comfortable with the pursuit of influence and power, not just achievement. Women must also get over their fear of risk and the pressure to be perfect. The fear of making mistakes can lead to missed opportunities. It is impossible to build power without taking risks and moving out of your comfort zone.

Women also need to improve another power play – relationship building. To advance in your career you must connect with influential people and seek them out for strategic advice. It is more than okay to fail. Setbacks are inevitable if you seek power.

Jill Flynn, Kathryn Heath and Mary Davis Holt (experts on women's leadership) believe that women who do not believe power is important are making a big mistake; managing your own power is not optional.[162] To improve power, they suggest two practical steps. Make a map of your corporate culture and chart the peer groups that have influence. Get to those people and understand their spheres of influence. Being aware of informal teams and alliances will help when you are trying to buy in or influence a decision. Cash in your chips and trade on your relationships. Campaign for your career. Women need to run for office positions by articulating a perspective, creating a platform, and lining up sponsors ... and then doing it all over again when the agenda changes.[163]

A 2019 study by Professor Sarah Arpin and colleagues concludes that women do not achieve their ambitions because they are not recognized for their efforts. Their study established a positive relationship between power and gratitude. "Because gratitude is predicated on recognition that others value oneself, power amplifies rather than undercuts feelings of gratitude."[164]

It turns out superwomen have these same issues. The paradox of women's power is in pop culture too. In "Bewitched Again: Supernaturally Powerful Women on Television: 1996-2011," Professor Julie D. O'Reilly writes that starting in 1996, U.S. television saw an influx of superhuman female characters who could materialize objects, like Sabrina, The Teenage Witch, to defeat evil like Buffy the Vampire Slayer, and have premonitions like Charmed's Phoebe.[165] She opines that supernaturally powerful women are powerful but not empowered. Her research of the TV shows reveals that these women often "reinforce the same hegemonic power structures they challenge." For example, in Bewitched, Samantha was married to Darrin, a mortal man, who disapproved of Samantha's use of magic and attempted to repress it. Samantha struggled during all eight seasons to be part of a normal, happy couple.

Jeannie, in "I Dream of Jeannie" was at her master's behest and frequently was put back in the bottle. Therefore, supernaturally powerful women are not as authoritative and liberated as one would expect. When she compares supernaturally powerful women to supernaturally powerful men, she finds that although the men and women face the same trials, the outcomes differ. When men face an authoritative institution, they are worthy opponents. Women, on the other hand, are portrayed as objects.

The extraordinary abilities of these women showed resistance to traditional gender roles, although these characters experienced infringements on their abilities in ways super-powered men did not. More recent characters also face constraints on their power. As a result, super-powers become a narrative technique to diminish these characters, a technique that began with television's first super powered woman - Samantha of Bewitched. O'Reilly posits that they all illustrate a paradox of women's power: are these characters ever truly powerful, much less super-powerful if they cannot use their abilities fully? The superwoman has endured as a metaphor for women trying to have it all; therefore, the travails of these television examples parallel those of their off-screen counterparts.

Is ambition, like boasting, also seen as a male priority? Do women lack ambition because being ambitious is not feminine? Dr. Anne Fels asks whether women do not exert their power because they lack the vision and the drive to see it through. She posits that because women are not recognized for work the way their male counterparts are and do not receive confirmation that their work is valuable, it is riskier to exert the kind of effort required to achieve one's ambition. In other words, they do not see success as worth it. She interviewed successful women who pushed personal recognition aside and gave it to others. They explained their success as a lucky instance and went so far as to say their success was "serendipitous."[166]

Women commonly build others up, even when they deserve to acknowledge themselves. Fels explains these women's deferments as their unconscious internalization of the idea that they must deflect attention to be feminine. Women, even powerful and successful women, think owning their success is unfeminine. She also notes that even though girls' and women's achievements, particularly in the academic sphere, frequently outstrip those of their male peers, they routinely underestimate their abilities.

The impact of this is profound. If you do not think the chances are great that you will reach a career goal, you will not attempt to reach it - even if the rewards are highly desirable.

How do ambition and raising a family relate? These days Fels believes the threat to ambitions comes at a later phase in a woman's life - when they have families and are advancing to more competitive positions in their work. Fels notes that women whose children have already grown up can act however they please because they have filled all their own requirements for being "feminine" - they have raised their children.

Yet, Sheryl Sandberg in her 2011 commencement speech at Barnard College warned the female graduates that if they decide to take less interesting, less meaningful paths in the name of "work-life balance" early on, then they will be very less likely to leave that career later - not because they don't want to work, but because their work doesn't challenge or compel them. She argued that women set themselves up for boring or drudging work by making such "leaving" decisions early and in small increments. Instead, Sandberg urged the women to "keep their feet on the pedal" until they reach a point where they must make decisions about work-life balance. She cited a report that women underestimate their successes and stated that men tend to overestimate their successes. Women on the other hand, are more likely to attribute their success to luck or serendipity or the help of others.[167]

What is the impact of self-esteem on power? In their 1992 article on Gender and Self Esteem, Robert Josephs and colleagues suggest that women are more likely than men to develop a collectivist, connected schema. Relations with other people, especially valued and important others, are crucial elements and are part of women's self-appraisal.

Men, on the other hand, are more likely to develop an individualist, independent, or autonomous model for themselves.

Do single career women avoid career-enhancing actions because these actions signal ambition and that may not be desirable to a man they may wish to marry? Professor of Economics Leonardo Bursztyn and colleagues in a field experiment of married and unmarried women found that while married and unmarried female MBA students performed similarly when their performance was unobserved by classmates (on exams and problem sets), unmarried women had lower participation grades and reported lower desired salaries and willingness to travel and work long hours on a real stakes placement questionnaire when they expected their classmates to see their preferences. Perhaps, the single women shifted the exercise of power toward something they think is more important and that is perceived as a different type of power.

What really holds women back at work? Princeton Professor Ann Marie Slaughter[168] opines that women have ambition, but they feel indispensable to their families. She believes that women left high profile career positions not because they could not take the work or were not committed enough, but because they valued their families more than work and thought someone else could take their place at work. Men, however, are more likely to think they are indispensable when in powerful positions.

She advocates for a workplace adjustment and offers solutions, such as changing the culture that rewards useless (arguable) long hours, scheduling in-person meetings during school days and evenings and instead turning office positions to remote ones where possible. In other words, it is the structure and the environment that is prohibiting women from having it all.

Author and relationship coach, Suzanne Venker, in a Fox News article, said "Should it be illegal to be a stay-at-home mom? Why feminists are so frustrated, "addresses the antipathy of feminists to traditional feminine pursuits such as homemaking and homeschooling. She quotes Sarrah le Marquand, an Australian feminist, "Rather than wail about the supposed liberation in a woman's right to choose to shun paid employment, we should make it a legal requirement that all parents of children of school-age or older are gainfully employed." Marquand fears that if women are not forced to enter the workplace, gender equality will never be achieved.[169]

Changes are needed in the work[170]place and COVID may be forcing us back to the pre-Industrial Revolution era when "work" and "life" were at home and not separate. Women's economic role in society was quite different before the Industrial Revolution moved the economy out of the home, separating home from the workplace As Dr. Maxine Berg wrote in her 1991 article, *Women's Work and the Industrial Revolution*, "The Industrial Revolution, traditionally associated with the late eighteenth and nineteenth centuries, has long been seen as the great historical turning point in the nature of women's working lives. For with it came a reorganization of the production process which separated the household from the workplace. A debate has raged among both feminists and historians since the early years of this century over the positive and negative impact of industrialization on women's workforce participation and status. Optimists have argued that industrialization and the factory brought gains in employment and higher wages which improved women's status within the family. Pessimists have argued that women's jobs were narrowed to less skilled and valued work and that women's social position was degraded by the decline of the household economy."

World War I and II had profound impacts too. Women were thrust from the home into the workplace. In a 1942 Social Security Bulletin,[171] the resource makes it clear that women going to work in factories for the first time were trained in courses in and outside the plants. Many women were trained in the factories in vestibule training schools. In strenuous jobs in which the direct replacement of male workers was not practicable, job break-down made the employment of women possible. Whenever careful consideration and thought were given to the problem of training, the employment of women in factories was highly successful.

This Bulletin also described how working mothers could achieve work-life balance. "Undoubtedly appeals to patriotism would cause many women to seek war employment. Nevertheless, some means will have to be found to relieve women homemakers of part of their family obligations before they can assume work outside the home. This problem has been met in some foreign countries through the establishment of community nurseries, staggered and part-time hours and other measures which enable women to meet home obligations and still seek employment. In addition to community nurseries in some industrial areas, various war firms in Great Britain have established creches in the plants for the care of children of pre-school age. Where facilities for such care are not available in the factory, arrangements are frequently made for neighbors to care for children of working mothers. Part-time shifts have been arranged in many plants, to give women sufficient time to attend to their family duties. Persons too old to take on full time employment are being taken back for part time work in retail shops to relieve the shortage of workers and to release younger workers, both men and women, for war work."[172]

Post war, many more women flooded the employment market and left their homes. In "Women Workers in 1960: Geographical Differences: Women's Bureau Bulletin No. 284 (1962): 1-26, the author writes, "Social and economic factors behind the remarkable advance in the number of women workers have been discussed frequently. They include the need of an expanding economy for additional workers in occupations employing women: the easing of household tasks by the use of modern appliances and equipment; the higher standard of living desired by our society; and changes in traditional attitudes toward women's work outside the home."

As more and more women entered the work force outside of the home, the issue of work-life balance grew. As University of Bombay Professor Shobba Sundaresan wrote[173] "the dynamics of the work environment have exerted enormous pressure on working women as they need to cope with virtually two full time jobs - one at the office and the other at home. To succeed in one environment working women are often called upon to make sacrifices in another, as each of the environments make different demands on them and have distinct norms to adhere to."[174]

Sundaresan concludes that the major consequences of poor work-life balance are high levels of stress and anxiety, disharmony at home, experiencing job burnout, and an inability to realize full potential. Women feel irritable and resentful, often due to their inability to balance work and family life.

Harvard Business School Professor Robin Ely posits that women were not held back because of trouble balancing the competing demands of work and family; men, too, suffered from the balance problem and nonetheless advanced. Women were held back because, unlike men, they were encouraged to make accommodations such as going part time and shifting to internally facing roles, which derailed their careers. The real culprit is the general culture of overwork that prevails in contemporary corporate culture, hurts both men and women, and locks gender inequality in place. Women pay higher professional costs." To solve this problem Ely posits we must reconsider what we are willing to allow the workplace to demand of all employees.[175]

COVID is, in fact, certainly changing the workplace and it may be bringing us back to a pre-Industrial (with a modern ZOOM twist) orientation. For many professionals who no longer commute there are many extra hours in the week. Working mothers are feeling the effect of juggling work and life (including child-care and the education of children) in the home. With men and women (and children) all working at home, the future will reset work-life balance. The lack of physical commuting, the increase in telecommuting and the division of labor will surely change. New ideas may come from this, such as the 4-day work week, more flexible worktimes and schedules, and an end to the stigma of permanently working remotely.

Jennifer Petriglieri in her Harvard Business Review, "How Dual Career Couples Can Work Through the Coronavirus Crisis"[176] acknowledges that "work is more stressful than usual as our face to face moves online, our organizations struggle to serve customers, and job security becomes uncertain, and so there is plenty of frustration and anxiety to take home. And now it *is* home. Our homes have become the spaces where we deal with these challenges. With no clear division of labor between paid work and housework, dual career couples are facing a host of new and unfamiliar challenges. How can both partners work productively under the same roof? Who gets to use the home office, and when? How can we avoid falling into the trap of overwork and burnout that is prevalent among home workers? How can we deal with each other's mildly annoying habits that when lived with 24/7 suddenly become bones of contention? And for those who are working parents, how do we keep the kids occupied and homeschooled with no friends, grandparents, or paid childcare givers to help?"

Petriglieri offers practical solutions to these questions and believes partners should address the following questions (based on an agreed timeline of perhaps three months). What matters most to you? What is the relative priority of your careers over the coming months? What are your parenting principles during this period? What do you need from each other to make all this work? What are the things that concern you the most?

Perhaps in this rapidly changing Post COVID world it is important to understand that this is not the time to be a lone wolf. As Professor Priscilla Claman suggests in her Harvard Business Review article, *Working Parents, Your Family Needs a Board of Directors*,[177]another practical solution is to establish a personal board of directors that you can consult with regularly to get advice and feedback on your work and career. She suggests that this will help you both at work and at home. The personal board of directors should include people who can help you think about personal issues and should comprise people you trust, have an interest in you and your family, and have experience or perspective to share. It should include a range of people from all different aspects of your life and include mentors whose networks do not overlap.

Her specific suggestions for whom to include on the board are: someone who shares your family's goals, one or more work colleagues who have families, working parents of children the same age as yours, working parents of children who are older than yours, parents with children who are younger than yours (to give perspective on the progress you have made), a parent you like and respect but who frequently disagrees with you, and someone who thinks you and your family are wonderful.

Once your board is assembled, Claman stresses it is important to stay in touch (perhaps through social media and pictures), thanking them for their friendship and support and letting them know how their advice worked out. Giving back to the group is also important. Claman acknowledges that you probably already have a group of these people in your orbit. Being intentional about what they mean and how they are organized will provide support to you as you navigate these tricky times.

It is important to figure out how to realize our own power. Canadian author, Heather Plett, in a 2014 blog post[178], "What if we were unafraid of our power?" writes that women have picked up a lot of messages that they should not be too confident, too powerful, too mystical, too shiny, too large, too expressive, too bossy, too strong, too creative, too wild, etc. She posits this is because woman's power is a dangerous thing. Too many women stepping into their own power would cause the world to shift and women themselves are afraid of holding that responsibility. It is also because patriarchy has worked long and hard to control and contain women's power, and it's because women are often their own worst enemies. She suggests that many women carry old stories about themselves with them and that it is when those stories are rewritten that power surfaces.

Capacity coach, Lisa Fabrega, in a blog post on her website, says "The confidence experiment: why women leaders fear being powerful and what they can do about it," also claims women fear being too confident, too direct, and too visible. She suggests changing this with some practical steps: accepting compliments proudly, agreeing with compliments, and speaking without apology.[179]

In her article, Why Women Are Afraid of their Power," published in *Medium*, author, Maya Yonika writes that women fear that if they tap into their own power they will disrupt their relationships. She is of the opinion that the antidote to this is for a woman to take responsibility for herself and quotes Marianne Williamson:

"Our deepest fear is not that we are inadequate. Our deepest fear is that we are powerful beyond measure. It is our light, not our darkness that most frightens us. We ask ourselves, 'Who am I to be brilliant, gorgeous, talented, fabulous?' Actually, who are you not to be? You are a child of God. Your playing small does not serve the world. There is nothing enlightened about shrinking so that other people will not feel insecure around you. We are all meant to shine, as children do. We were born to make manifest the glory of God that is within us. It's not just in some of us; it's in everyone. And as we let our own light shine, we unconsciously give other people permission to do the same. As we are liberated from our own fear, our presence automatically liberates others."[180]

# Chapter 8:

# Women's Betrayal of Women

**"There is a special place in hell for women who do not help other women."**

*-Madeline Albright*
*(keynote speech at Celebrating Inspiration luncheon with WNBA's All-Decade Team 2006)*

**"Oh, how I prefer the honest violence of men, who will bash in another man's skull and be done, to the thousand shallow cuts of women's malice."**

*— Candace Fleming, Fatal Throne*

The popular nursery rhyme

*What are little boys made of?*
*What are little boys made of?*
*Snips and snails*
*And puppy-dogs› tails*
*That's what little boys are made of*

*What are little girls made of?*
*What are little girls made of?"*
*Sugar and spice*
*And everything nice*
*That's what little girls are made of*

Is a myth.

Not all women help women. Not all women play well in the sandbox. Some women want to hurt other women professionally – and succeed.

While feminists have generally depicted women as empathetic and caring creatures, victims of male aggression and dominance Phyllis Chesler, a psychologist and well-known feminist contends instead that women give as good as they get, especially toward each other.[181] Her book, *Woman's inhumanity to Woman,*[182] *which* includes the work of 60 writers and researchers who have addressed "the shadow side of female-female relationships," offers scientific and historical evidence on female violence.

Among primates, evolutionary psychologists have found females often bid for alpha status by trying to sabotage the reproductive cycles of their sisters. Mother lemurs and chimps have been known to kill and cannibalize their competitors' babies.

On the human side, Japanese, Chinese, and Indian mothers-in-law beat their son's wives, whom they treat more like slaves than daughters. Genital mutilation in Africa, honor killings in Islamic countries, burnings over dowry disputes in India all take place against women with the support of women.

More commonly, females battle each other by resorting to "social aggression"- gossip, manipulation, and back-stabbing. Research shows that nastiness starts early. Schoolgirls use their social skills to jockey for status within a clique and when slighted, their grudges and resentments last a lot longer than those of boys.

Although men are more often guilty of physical violence, women's tendency to use indirect aggression can lead them to oppose each other in more destructive and hurtful ways. Indirect aggression can take the form of shunning and malicious gossip. This could be a result of women feeling they have to compete against each other for token "female" positions. One study found, for example, that female economists were more likely than their male counterparts to reject the proposals of women for National Science Foundation funding.

Chesler notes that things are no better in office settings, where women obey the dictates of "gender standards" and some female managers pretend to be caring mother figures in order to suppress dissent and demands for money, while others act like "male impersonators."

Women often find it difficult to acknowledge female aggression because these are not socially acceptable traits for women to have and because a woman's best friends and confidants are usually other women.[183] Most women rely on a family of female best friends.

In addition, women, like men, have internalized sexist beliefs. Women often have higher and different expectations for other women than women have for men. They also have more compassion for male failure or imperfection than female failure.

To move forward, Chesler writes, women must acknowledge the painful truth that women are normally aggressive and competitive, and oppressed women are very angry (and therefore tend to take anger out on each other). This acknowledgement may help a woman to become more realistic about what to expect from other women and become clearer about her own limitations as well.

Other suggestions:

- Honor your own ambition and the ambition of other women.
- Support strong women who are different from you, not only weak women who agree with you and therefore do not threaten you.
- Be strong enough to take criticism.
- Learn to express your anger and not hold a grudge.
- Ask for what you want and ask for it directly, rather than waiting for someone to guess what it is you want.
- If you don't get what you want, don't blame yourself, give up, disconnect, or become enraged.
- Do not punish or sabotage another woman whom you may envy or fear by slandering her or by turning other women against her.
- If a woman has slandered or sabotaged you, talk to her about it directly, deal with it quickly and move on.
- Treat women respectfully. Cultivate the concept of an "honorable opponent" rather than automatically demonizing a competitor.

Given the nurturing and collaborative nature of women's relationships, what motivates women to commit betrayal and sabotage? Studies suggest the answer may lie in two factors: One is women's need for equality in relationships. Women's friendships are based on a flattened hierarchy in which friends have equal status. Maintaining equality is a balancing game. If status changes (marriage, new baby, new job, promotion, weight loss, gain in wealth or popularity) disequilibrium may occur and the friendship may deteriorate. Unless the friends can re-equalize their status, the friendship may end. If neither woman feels threatened, they can remain friends.

The second factor is women's early socialization in dealing with conflict. Traditionally, girls are socialized to avoid overt conflict. They are taught to be nice, cooperate, and get along with others. When girls disagree, they quit and are likely to use passive aggressive behaviors or indirect aggression (i.e. malicious gossiping, staring, giggling, ridiculing, writing anonymous notes, forming cliques).

These passive-aggressive behaviors learned in childhood are likely to continue in adulthood and assume the form of sabotage. Triggers for sabotage include the new dynamic that is created when one woman has the power to bestow or take away something desired by the other (and the mutual reciprocity of the friendship has a new dynamic), when women are competing for the same position or promotion, when one woman is promoted as supervisor of another, when one woman in a group assumes a leadership role (and the other woman feels inadequate).[184]

Sociologist Marianne Cooper[185] posits there are two dominant cultural forces about the role women in play in women helping other women advance at work: the Righteous Woman (who holds the ideal belief that women have a distinct moral obligation to have one another's backs) and the Queen Bee (who undermines other women instead of using her power to help women advance). Both these stereotypes fuel a double standard - that conflict between men is normal, but conflict between women is dysfunctional. When men battle it out, they are engaging in healthy competition and vigorous debate. When women do the same thing, they are "mean girls" in a catfight. One study found that when a conflict took place between two women coworkers, people expected the consequences to be negative and long lasting - that the women would want revenge. When, however the same conflict happened between two men or a man and a woman, people thought the relationship could be more easily repaired.

Evidence suggests acting as a Queen Bee is not about being a prima donna, but instead a product of what scholars call a "value threat." Value threats exist when there are negative stereotypes of women in highly masculinized workplaces, stereotypes that women who manage to make it must constantly fight to hold their own positions, and this may shape their willingness to help other women.

Women may not support other women if there is any question about these women's qualifications because they don't want to do anything that might fuel the negative stereotypes. Cooper notes that calling a woman a "Queen Bee" is its own form of devaluation designed to denigrate and marginalize women in leadership. It is ironical that Queen Bee has come to mean this in human culture because in actual honeybee colonies the queen bee's survival is 100% dependent on the aid she receives from her colony of entirely female bees - whether they are worker bees or nurse bees. The honeybee colony mode exists on the premise of female bees using their own power to help the queen bee maintain her power. It is more of a mutual exchange of power than an oppressive power. The power of the queen bee in nature is contingent on the power of the collective.

In personality psychology *the locus of control* refers to the extent to which individuals believe they can control events affecting them. That locus can be external (a person's decisions and life are controlled by environmental factors they cannot influence) or internal (a person believes she can control her life).[186]

Research confirms women are more likely to have an external locus of control. When a woman with a more external locus of control, who has a lack of confidence in her own abilities and who has internalized messages about other women, enters a competitive male-dominated workplace, her dark, toxic side can be triggered by the increased scrutiny that women experience in the workplace. Female rivalry is fueled by a workplace culture that does not provide a level playing field for women. This sets women up to compete.

What happens when the dark side of that woman is turned on you and you are her target? Psychologist Bonnie Marcus suggests that you should then detach emotionally, build a power network to protect your reputation, find a sponsor and/or mentor, strengthen your confidence, control your career destiny, and be a role model for collaboration over competition.

Women cannot control other people's bad behavior. Women can only control their own reactions to that behavior. Focusing on the things we can control to protect our reputations and remaining positive and productive will help to stay on track.

Some women snub women in the workplace and some women deliberately hold women back. Sometimes it is intentional and sometimes it is far more subtle. And that can happen when women are not supportive of other women in the workplace, when they do not share their experiences and provide a support network.

Anne Welsh McNulty, a leader in the financial sector and a philanthropist"[187] writes that her experiences from being a rookie accountant to a managing director at an investment bank taught her that conversations between women have massive benefits for the individual and the organization. As a first-year accountant in a large accounting firm she kept asking the only woman senior to her to have lunch. The woman finally told her, "Look there's only room for one female partner here. You and I are not going to be friends."

McNulty points to a 2016 study in the Academy of Management Journal that senior level women who champion younger women today are more likely to get negative performance reviews.

In contrast, in her book *Executive Presence: The Missing Link Between Merit and Success,*[188] Sylvia Ann Hewlett notes that men are 46% more likely to have a higher-ranking advocate in the office and this makes an increasing difference in representation as they proceed up the corporate organizational chart.

Worse than being snubbed by the women above her, McNulty says, was the lack of communication between women at her level. At the end of her first year she was shocked and surprised that all four of the other women who started with her had quit or been fired. She was shocked because the women had not talked among themselves enough to understand what was happening. She had had difficult experiences with men who criticized her, commented on her looks, or flatly said she did not deserve to work there, but she had no idea other women were experiencing similar challenges. They had all expected their performance to be judged as objectively as their clients' books and did not realize the importance of banding together until it was too late.

McNulty resolved that this should not happen again to other women and she took it into her own hands, as her career advanced, to host women-only lunches and open channels of communication. She created an open-door policy and shared her own experiences. Open communication improved the flow of information and relieved tension and anxiety. The women understood that they were not alone when facing challenges. Sponsorship and mentorship by women of women was critical to lifting each other up and creating a culture of support. She notes that professional women's networks like Ellevate Network, Ellevest, and WIE (Women Inspiration and Enterprise) that provide support to women who struggle with the issues they face are very important but they do not replace the power of internal sponsorship and mentorship.

In conclusion, it is important to understand and acknowledge that women do compete with each other. Some women hold other women back, some women snub other women, and some women want to hurt other women. It is not just men who can sabotage women. Women can sabotage women too. As women continue to advance in the workplace they, too will become more aggressive about their positions. Competition can bring out the best and the worst in all of us. It is important to be aware of our own actions and think about what, why, and how we compete and what, why, and how we collaborate.

# Chapter 9:

# Men Sabotaging Women

**"Men are beasts, and even beasts don't behave as they do."**

*-Brigitte Bardot*

Some men sabotage women. Why? Fear? Tradition? Culture? Because they can? Insecurity? I remember shortly after graduating from law school a friend missed an important job interview because her boyfriend found the letter inviting her to interview at a certain time and destroyed it before she read it. I was very confused as to why anyone would do that, and I was confused as to why she stayed with him - but she did. The dance between men and women has always been complicated.

Do men sabotage women in the workplace? Sure – sometimes. And when they do, is it conscious? Unconscious? This is a conversation that has evolved as more women have entered the work force and attained leadership positions. In 1977 the Harvard Business Review published an article, "Two Women, Three Men on a Raft," by Robert Schrank. It was republished in 1994 as part of an anthology of HBR articles on women and work, entitled "Reach for the Top: Women and the Changing Facts of Work Life," edited by Nancy A. Nichols. In the article Shrank described his Outward Bound "survival training" experience in which the 20 participants were divided into four groups to travel down the Rogue River in Oregon. His raft was the only one that ended up with two women and three men. All participants were anxious and fearful, and his group created a nice, supportive atmosphere.

Each raft team member was to take a turn at ruddering the raft and issuing commands. They were taught how to recognize a rapid's tongue (entrance), how to avoid "sleepers" (hidden rocks) and how to ride the "haystacks" (choppy waves) as they came out of the rapids. They were taught how to chop their paddles into the waves as they rode into haystacks. The raft had no seat belts, so unless they chopped down hard, they would be tossed out of the raft. At night they would camp. During the day they would ride the rapids.

Schrank noted that when either woman tried to carry the supplies, one of the men would yell out, "Let me hold it; it is too heavy for you." The men on the team pitched the tarpaulins at night, the women made the beds, cleaned the ground, and arranged the sleeping bags. As they proceeded down the river, the women were unsure of their abilities and the men solely but subtly began to take charge.

The teamwork began to unravel. On the fifth day down the river the woman team member at the helm did not give a command and the raft hit a boulder and flipped over. The woman decided she no longer wanted to helm the boat. The other woman then joined in and said she, too would not take the helm. Their raft came in last.

Schrank, back in his office after the experience, reflected on what really happened and concluded that not only had he been unhappy with a woman as a helmsperson; he and the other male teammates had subconsciously, by habit, undermined the women. When one of the other men was in charge, Schrank felt comfortable, supportive, and worked to help him be better. When a woman was at the helm he seemed to direct his anxiety at the experience to getting her replaced by one of the men on the raft.

Schrank wrote that the most revealing part of the experience was not the power relationship between the sexes; it was how the men unconsciously or automatically responded to protect their power from female encroachment. The men actively tried to sabotage the women's ability to lead. They were unconsciously building on each woman's doubts about herself with negative reinforcement of her leadership role. This increased the woman's doubts about herself as leader. He also noted that for each of them their lifelong conditioning that a woman ought to be a passive sweet thing came in to play and eventually both gave up the helm because men "do it better."

Schrank, on further reflection, noted that this did not just happen in the wilderness. It happened in corporate America when women entered leadership positions (except, perhaps, for organizations that were formed by women). There was a cultural way of granting power to men. To the macho male it was his role to take care of a woman, particularly if she faced danger and he should not yield that power. In addition, because organizations were usually organized in a pyramid, the moving up process meant someone was squeezed out and men were threatened by women taking their roles. Women were in trouble because the lack of support they received from men was reinforced by others as a collective activity.

He concluded that women trying to navigate most organizations might find them more complex than the Rogue River, but women should look out for similar hazards. In the workplace the men were the sleepers and the chutes who, when their power was threatened, would pull the women down.

Schrank reassessed his Rogue River trip 17 years later and reflected that his initial thoughts were right. The workplace has changed and he strongly believes that "women have fallen short of their goals because we (men) underestimate men's need to maintain their power. Even if all the rules on equal opportunity are followed our "underneath" power will continue to keep women from succeeding.

"When females threaten to move into power positions, men are threatened twice; first that they will lose authority over women, and second, that they will lose the game."

Faith Wohl, commenting on Schrank's reflections, notes that the raft lost its competitive position because management failed to create an environment in which a diverse team could achieve trust and mutual respect. She opines that today's rapids demand highly responsive team members who can act alone or together without anyone to lead them.

In 1997 Sheila Wellington, the then president of Catalyst, commented on Schrank's thoughts by noting that since the river trip, women have learned a few things and the world no longer revolves around the physical strength of the male hunter. Rather, today's successful business "warrior" is marked by an awareness of the changing world and leadership and team building skills that rely on brains, not brawn. Women are better educated now and have entered the ranks of corporate management. Perhaps, she posits, some of the men have changed too.

In 1997 Eleanor Peterson, one of the woman on the Rogue River raft, commented on Schrank's thoughts and said that when she first read it 17 years earlier, she was angry at the game the men played and angry at her own failure to realize what was going on. She writes that in 1997 she would not let this happen because she would take the helm and the responsibility no matter how frightened she was. And she would make the men give it to her. She was forceful. "You cannot bring about change politely. You have to be tough. You have to be rude. Before the civil rights movement, people said to blacks, "Don't try to move too fast." But after 100 years of waiting, they lost patience and so took change into their own hands. Women must do the same".

James Grubman, a well-known psychologist, notes that in the workplace a difficulty for both men and women is having a good internal model of female power. Men tend to have a competitive or adversarial view of power where there is a winner and a loser (or a winner and everyone one else loses). There is also a dominant/submissive or aggressor/victim model in different variations. Men experience women displaying or exerting power within that model, so if there is female power, men feel threatened as losing.

Perhaps a healthier power model is one of collaboration, not competition. In collective societies and cultures collaboration is much more common, understood, and modeled. In individualist cultures such as the United States collaboration is advocated but not modeled much.

So, men interpret that women exerting female power are "trying to take over," or that the "men have to submit" to a strong woman.

Many women unfortunately believe the same thing. It is a win/lose game rather than a win/win game. Those rare men who understand and value collaboration have a much easier time accepting and welcoming women who are powerful, although if a woman seems to be exerting competitive power rather than collaborative power, it evokes either a competitive response or pushback.

Finding the intersection of female power with collaborative style may be optimal, but in very individualist cultures this can be difficult. Aside from the common behavioral issues around men tolerating women exerting power, a hidden but major factor for both men and women is having a good internal template of what effective benevolent power looks like.

The feminist movement started with the concept that power over women, domination or control is implicitly masculine. Feminism's fourth wave began around 2006 and drives the #MeToo and Times Up Movements, with the goal of holding powerful men accountable for their behavior toward women. Tarana Burke, an activist from the Bronx started the #MeToo movement in 2006 to raise awareness of sexual harassment and sexual abuse by having girls and women share their stories. The movement dramatically expanded with the 2017 Harvey Weinstein sexual allegations. Journalist Ronan Farrow took on the "casting couch" powerful practice of men exchanging sex for movie roles.[189] With Farrow's reporting and New York Times reporters, Jodi Kantor and Megan Twohey's book, "She Said,"[190] a groundswell began, resulting in the sentencing of Weinstein, and many other prominent men, such as Roger Ailes, Charlie Rose and Matt Lauer losing their long-held jobs, power, and privilege.

But as time has gone on there has been a backlash to this movement too. Tim Bower, in a 2019 Harvard Business Review article, "The #MeToo Backlash," wrote that in the wake of #MeToo many people expected men to become more reluctant to engage with women at work in certain ways - even though such activities could be crucial to women's advancement.[191]

A 2019 follow up survey revealed an even bigger backlash. Nineteen percent of men said they were reluctant to hire attractive women, 21% said they were reluctant to hire women for jobs involving close interpersonal interactions with men (for example, jobs with travel) and 27% of men said they avoided one-on-one meetings with female colleagues. Rachel Strum, a researcher on the project, said this is all actually a step backward for women.[192]

Journalist Kristina Monllos writes that women are now missing opportunities. "I feel like it shifted from sexual misconduct to sexual exclusion. Women are still feeling uncomfortable in that we're still being judged for our gender - just in an entirely different way."[193]

Carl Fremont, CEO of Quigley-Simpson noted that by separating teams by gender we do not get the best thinking and are condoning bad behavior, rather than establishing the way we build respect and trust among co-workers.[194]

Kim Elsesser[195] writes that the reluctance to hire women joins a long list of behaviors at work that have been negatively impacted by #MeToo. 2019 research from LeanIn.org revealed that 60% of male managers were uncomfortable participating in job related activities with women, such as mentoring, working alone together or socializing. The Pew Research Center found 51% of employees reported feeling that #MeToo made interactions with the opposite sex harder at work.

There is also a legal backlash. In her 2020 article journalist Madison Pauly writes that while it is well known that powerful men have preemptively quashed accusations with payoffs and nondisclosure agreements, less well known is that dozens of men who claim they are victims of false allegations have sued their accusers for defamation for speaking out publicly.[196]

On the other hand, reporter Anna North states that good things have occurred too.[197] States are banning nondisclosure agreements that cover sexual harassment. States are introducing protections for more workers. New York, for example, expanded its sexual harassment law to cover independent contractors. The Time's Up Legal Defense Fund has helped 3,600 people obtain legal representation in sexual harassment lawsuits, which can be prohibitively expensive. Congress has reformed the process for staffers reporting sexual harassment. Some survivors are getting financial restitution.

And Americans have changed how they think about power. North posits that one of the biggest effects of the movement has been to show Americans and people around the world how widespread sexual harassment, assault, and other misconduct is. Because of that, people learned they were not alone and people who had never had cause to think about sexual harassment before suddenly saw how much it had affected their coworkers, children, parents, and friends. She concludes that the #MeToo movement has been a driving force behind how people are thinking about power now - who has it, who does not have it and how those with more power are trying to control those with less power.

# CONCLUSION

Power is in each and every one of us regardless of what year it is, what the era is, what the culture is, what the political climate is, what the laws are, or what our individual circumstances are.

Power is imbedded in the ageless wisdom of our souls. It cannot be taken away from you or me without our permission.

Each of us owns the power to compose our own life, to earn our own money (or not), to have a career (or not), to marry (or not), to have children (or not), to worship (or not), and to collaborate (or not).

Our use of our power is an individual responsibility. We owe it to ourselves to explore our power, enjoy our power, make mistakes with our power, learn from our power, and stand up with power.

It is up to each of us to decide if we wish to use our power, how we choose to use our power, how we maintain our power, how we protect our power, and when we choose to use our power.

It is up to each of us to decide if we want to hone the behavioural skills that allow us to focus and enhance our power.

Our use of power is not static. It is evolutionary. The choices we make about our own power will change as our lives change.

It is up to each of us to step into our own power. We do not need permission from anyone to do this.

It is our individual responsibility to value ourselves, to protect ourselves and our contributions in order to accomplish great things in the world, and in so doing to protect ourselves, those we love, and the institutions we care about.

# Endnotes


1 Yorio, Kara, "PBS Looks at Modern Women's History," *The Record (Bergen County, NJ)*, 26 February 2013.

2 Blakemore, Erin, "Five Things to Know About the Declaration of Sentiments," *Smithsonian Magazine*, 8 June 2016.

3 "Declaration of Sentiments and Resolutions" Seneca Falls Convention, 1848.

4 Blakemore, Erin, "Five Things to Know About the Declaration of Sentiments."

5 Blakemore, Erin, "Five Things to Know About the Declaration of Sentiments."

6 Mabretti, Catherine Cole, "The Burden of the Ballot: The Woman's Anti-Suffragette Movement", American Heritage, 1978.

7 Mabretti, Catherine Cole, "The Burden of the Ballot."

8 Mabretti, Catherine Cole, "The Burden of the Ballot."

9 de Beauvoir, Simone. *The Second Sex,* France 1949, released in USA in 1953 and Grady, Constance, "The waves of feminism, and why people keep fighting over them, explained." *Vox.com*. 7 July 2018.

10 Simons, Margaret A. and Marybeth Timmermann, *Feminist Writings: The Beauvoir Series*, University of Illinois Press (2015).

11 Friedan, Betty, *The Feminine Mystique*, Norton (1963). See also Carmody, Deirdre, "Feminists Scored by Betty Friedan", *The New York*

*Times*, 1972., Churchill, Lindsey Blake. "The Feminine Mystique." *Encyclopaedia Britannica*, 2019, and Fetters, Ashley. "4 Big Problems With The Feminine Mystique", *The Atlantic*, 4 February 2013.

12 Farb, Cris. "New Again: Gloria Steinem", *Interview Magazine*. 8 March 2017.

13 Carmody, Deirdre, "Feminists Scored by Betty Friedan", for the discussion of Friedan/Steinem/Abzug.

14 Fields, Suzanne. "Leader Who Transformed the Image of a Conservative Woman.", *The Washington Times (Washington D.C.)*. October 30, 2005. For the discussion of Friedan/Schlafly see also Critchlow, Donald T. "*Phyllis Schlafly and Grassroots Conservatism: A Woman's Crusade*", Princeton Press (2005) and Foussianes, Chloe. "How Phyllis Schlafly, an Anti-ERA Conservatist Activist, Left an Enduring Mark on the Republican Party". *Town and Country Magazine*. 18 April 2020.

15 Farb, Carolyn. "New Again: Gloria Steinem", *Interview Magazine*. 8 March 2017 for a discussion of Steinem/Schlafly/Palin/Bachmann.

16 Michaelson, Judith. "Steinem's New "Marilyn" Looks at Vulnerability". *Los Angeles Times*. 10 December 1986., Steinem, Gloria, "*MARILYN*". Photographs by George Barris. Henry Holt & Company. Fine Communications 1997., and Trilling, Diana, "Please Don't Make Me a Joke", *New York Times*, 21 December 1986 for a discussion of Gloria Steinem and Marilyn Monroe.

17 For a discussion of the feminist waves see Cook, Sarah Gibbard, "Feminists Differ in Second and Third Waves". *Wiley Online Library*, 2014. See also Ehrenreich, Barbara. "Save Me the Despair". *The Progressive*, Vol. 73, Issue 12. December 2019., Friedlin, Jennifer, "Second and Third Wave Feminists Clash Over the Future.", *Women's ENews*, 2002., Gilley, Jennifer. "Writings of the Third Wave: Young Feminists in Conversation." Reference & Users Service Quarterly 44, no. 3 (2005): 187-98 and Grady, Constance, "The waves of feminism, and why people keep fighting over them, explained." *Vox*.com. 7 July 2018.

18 Williams, Joanna, "*Women v. Feminism: Why We All Need Liberating from the Gender Wars*". Emerald Publishing Ltd. 2017. See also Williams, Joanna, "Fourth Wave Feminism: Why No One Escapes". *The American Conservative*, 4 Sep. 2018.

19 The works of Edith B. Gelles are fundamental to the understanding of Abigail Adams. See Freeman, Jay. Review of Abigail

and John: Portrait of A Marriage, by Edith B. Gelles. *American Library Association* 105, No. 15:16 (January 2009)., Gelles, Edith B. "Domesticity and the American Revolution". The New England Quarterly, Vol. 52, No. 4 (Dec. 1979) pp 500-521., Gelles, Edith B. *"Abigail Adams: A Writing Life"*. Routledge 2002 and Gelles, Edith B. *"Portia: The World of Abigail Adams"*, Indiana University Press, 1992. The letters of Abigail and John Adams referred to in this Chapter were identified and quoted in Gelles works.

20 Abigail Adams, "Remember the Ladies", March 31, 1776 Letter.

21 Hass, Nancy. "Gloria Steinem Still Wants More." *Newsweek* 15 August 2011.

22 Gelles, Edith B. *"Abigail Adams: A Writing Life"*. Routledge 2002.

23 Gelles, Edith B. *"Portia: The World of Abigail Adams"*, Indiana University Press, 1992.

24 Ellis, Joseph J. *First Family: Abigail and John*. New York: Alfred A. Knopf (2010).

25 Blake, Miranda, "What Mrs. America Got Right and Wrong About Phyllis Schlafly", *The Los Angeles Times*, 24 April 2020.

26 Dwilson, Stephanie Dube, "Phyllis Schlafly's Husband, Fred Schlafly: Who Was He in Real Life?", *heavy.com* 22 April 2020.

27 See Critchlow, Donald T. *"Phyllis Schlafly and Grassroots Conservatism: A Woman's Crusade"*. Princeton Press (2005). See also Foussianes, Chloe. "How Phyllis Schlafly, an Anti-ERA Conservatist Activist, Left an Enduring Mark on the Republican Party". *Town and Country Magazine*. 18 April 2020.

28 Foussianes, Chloe, "How Phyllis Schlafly, an Anti-ERA Conservatist Activist, Left an Enduring Mark on the Republican Party".

29 Ziwica, Kristine, "There's a Case to be Made for Feminist Marriage- and Here's Why.", *ABC News*, 26 Sept. 2019 for a discussion of the marriage of Amelia Earhart and George Putnam.

30 Bonos, Lisa, "How Ruth Bader Ginsburg's "marriage of equals" has inspired her many fans.", *The Washington Post*, 23 September 2020.

31 Foussianes, Chloe, "How Ruth Bader Ginsburg's Late Husband, Marty, Helped Her Reach Her Potential", *Town & Country Magazine*, 19 September 2020.

32 Greenspan, Rachel E., "The Only Person I Have Ever Loved. Inside Ruth Bader Ginsburg's History-Shaping Marriage of Equals", *Time*, 19 September 2020.

33 Foussianes, Chloe, "How Ruth Bader Ginsburg's Late Husband, Marty, Helped Her Reach Her Potential".

34 Williams, Marjorie. "Barbara's Backlash", *Vanity Fair Magazine*, August 1992.

35 Bennetts, Leslie. "First Lady in Waiting". *Vanity Fair Magazine*, December 2007.

36 Iowa State University, "Wives Have Greater Power in marriage Problem-solving Behavior, According to Study", *Science Daily*, 2007.

37 Baer, Drake, "Turns Out That The Husband's Job is Probably The Best Predictor of Divorce", *www.thecut.com*, 28 July 2016.

38 Vincenty, Samantha. "4 Reasons Husbands Feel Like They Hate Their Wives", *Oprah Magazine*. 31 July 2019.

39 Gardner, Jr. Ralph. "Alpha Women, Beta Men". *New York Magazine*. 7 November 2003.

40 Byrne, Alison and Julian Barling. "Does a Woman's High-Status Career Hurt Her Marriage? Not if Her Husband Does the Laundry." *Harvard Business Review*, 2017.

41 For the discussion by Barbara Corcoran of her marriage see Gardner, Jr. Ralph. "Alpha Women, Beta Men". *New York Magazine*. 7 November 2003.

42 Knowledge@Wharton, "High-powered Women and Supportive Spouses: Who's in Charge and of What?", knowledge@wharton 7 November 2012.

43 Gillett, Rachel, "Power Couples Who Stay Together Have 9 Things in Common", *Business Insider*. 23 October 2017.

44 Petriglieri, Jennifer. *Couples That Work: How Dual Career Couples Can Thrive In Love and Work*. Harvard Business Review Press. October 8, 2019.

45 Luscombe, Belinde. *Marriageology: The Art and Science of Staying Together*. Random House, May 21, 2019.

46 Los, Agata. "Collective Unconscious: Carl Jung's prophetic ideas on our shared human heritage." *Neuroscience from Underground*, 2019.

47 Shinoda Bolen, Jean. *Goddesses in Everywoman: Powerful Archetypes in Women's Lives*. Harper, 2014.

48 Straub, Gail. *Returning to My Mother's House: Taking Back the Wisdom of the Feminine*. High Point, 2008.

49 Riggio, Ronald E. Ph.D. "Women's Intuition: Myth or Reality?" *Psychology Today*. 14 July 2019.

50 Austen, Ashleigh, "Science Confirms women's intuition is a real thing." *The New York Post*, 6 June 2017.

51 Schultz, Dr. Mona and Dr. Christianne Northrup, *The New Feminine Brain: Developing Your Intuitive Genius*. Atria Books 2006.

52 Huston, Therese. *How Women Decide: What's True, What's Not, and What Strategies Spark the Best Choices*. Houghton Mifflin Harcourt. 2016.

53 Huston, Therese. *How Women Decide: What's True, What's Not, and What Strategies Spark the Best Choices*.

54 Samra, Ravjinder "Female doctors show more empathy, but at a cost to their mental well-being". *The Conversation*, 2018.

55 Olmos, David. "When watching others in pain, women's brains show more empathy." *UCLA Newsroom*, 2019. Christov-Moore, Leonardo and Marco Iacoboni, "Sex differences in somatomotor representations of other's pain: a permutation-based analysis". *Brain Structure and Function* 224 (2019); 937-947.

56 Sacks M.D., Alexandra. "Reframing "Mommy Brain", *The New York Times*, 2018.

57 Gomez-Carvajal, A. et. al. "The unique social sense of puerperium: Increased empathy and *Schadenfreude* in parents of newborns." *Nature, Scientific Report* 10, no. 5760 (2020).

58 University of Cambridge, "Empathy and Engineering: Can our brain type explain the gender gap in STEM subjects and careers?" *University of Cambridge*. 2016.

59 Samra, Ravjinder "Female doctors show more empathy, but at a cost to their mental well-being". *The Conversation*, 2018 and Wallace, Jennifer. "Being empathetic is good, but it can hurt your health." *The Washington Post*. 2017.

60 Samra, Ravjinder "Female doctors show more empathy, but at a cost to their mental well-being".

61 Fray, Penny. "Welcome to the Eve-Olution; How Empathy, Emotional Intelligence and Traditional Female Traits are Helping Women Get Promoted", *Daily Post* (Liverpool), England, 14 April 2004.

62 Bowes, Barbara. "Empathy is the New Leadership Skill. A Contradiction to the Long Standing Image of a Good Leader", *Winnipeg Free Press*, 3 March 2018.

63 Bowes, Barbara. "Empathy is the New Leadership Skill. A Contradiction to the Long Standing Image of a Good Leader".

64 Shelley Taylor's work in this area is of critical importance. See Taylor, Shelley E. *The Tending Instinct: How Nurturing is Essential for Who We Are and How We Live.* New York, Henry Holt, 2002.

and see Taylor, Shelley E., Laura Cousino Klein, Brian P. Lewis, Tara L. Gruenewald, Regan A.R. Gurung and John A. Updegraff, University of California, Los Angeles, "Biobehavioural Response to Stress in Females: Tend-and-Befriend, Not Fight- or- Flight.", *Psychological Review*, 2000, Vol. 107, No. 3, 411-429.

65 George, Bill and Andrew N. McLean, "Oprah!", Harvard Business School Case Study, 9-405-087, 11, April 2007.

66 Jesmok, Janet. "Guiding Lights: Feminine Judgment and Wisdom in Malory's "Morte D'Arthur"", *Arthuriana* 19, no. 3 (2009) : 34-42.

67 De Tocqueville, Alexis. "Education of Young Women in the United States" and "How the Americans Understand the Equality of the Sexes". In *Democracy in America*, Vol. II. Project Gutenberg, 2013.

68 Id.

69 For a discussion of the impact of the Flappers see "How Flappers Redefined Womanhood (Hint: It involved jazz, liquor and sex)." *www.history.com*. See also Park, Soohyun "Flapper Fashion in the Context of Cultural Changes of America in the 1920s.", *Masters Thesis Submitted to Graduate Faculty in Liberal Studies CUNY NY* 2014; Rosenberg, Jennifer, "Flappers in The Roaring Twenties", *thoughtco.com*, 25 March 2020; Simon Linda, "Flappers Took the Country by Storm, But Did They Ever Truly Go Away", *Smithsonian Magazine*, September 2017 and Wikipedia, "Flapper".

70 Davis, Angela Yvonne, *Blues Legacies and Black Feminism: Gertude Ma Rainey, Bessie Smith and Billie Holiday,* Vintage, 1999.

71 For a very comprehensive study on the impact Madonna has had on culture see the exhaustive article, *Wikipedia,* "Cultural Impact of Madonna".

72 Pettigrew, Tina and Johanna Pulgarin, "Why Female Role Models Matter." *ForbesWoman* 12 March 2016. See also Marcus, Bonnie, "Want to be Successful? Find a Strong Female Role Model"., *ForbesWoman,* 29 March 2017.

73 Wikipedia.

74 Emanzadeh, Arash, "Women's Day and Female Role Models. The need for role models in the context of a sexist society." *Psychology Today,* 5 March 2019.

75 Emanzadeh, Arash, "Women's Day and Female Role Models. The need for role models in the context of a sexist society."

76 Marcus, Bonnie, "Want to be Successful? Find a Strong Female Role Model"., *ForbesWoman,* 29 March 2017.

77 Gerdeman, Dina. "Kids of Working Moms Grow Into Happy Adults". *Harvard Business Review.* 16 July 2018.

78 Shecancodeblog, "Role Models Are Key in Gender and Diversity- Especially in Tech and Engineering. *Shecancode.* 2 September 2019. See also "Lack of Female Role Models Driving Women Away from STEM Careers", *www.teiss.co.uk,* A Study by Kapersky Labs. 2019.

79 Peiss, Kathy L. "American Women and the Making of Modern Consumer Culture.", *The Journal for Multi Media History,* Volume 1, Number 1- Fall 1998.

80 Peiss, Kathy L. "American Women and the Making of Modern Consumer Culture."

81 Peiss, Kathy L. "American Women and the Making of Modern Consumer Culture."

82 Lahart, Justin and Laura Forman, "The Buck Stops Here: Accounting for Women's Spending Power.", *The Wall Street Journal,* 7 September 2019. See also Nelson, Amy "Women Drive Majority of Consumer Purchasing and It's Time to Meet Their Needs", *Inc. Magazine,*17 July 2019; Silverstein, Michael J. and Kate Sayre,

"The Female Economy", *Harvard Business Review,* September 2009.

83 Id.

84 Gilpin, Jamie, "Women are building the brands we've always wanted.", *sproutsocial.com,* 12 March 2019.

85 Mintel.com "The Evolution of Marketing to Women", *mintel.com,* 8 March 2019.

86 "Women Pioneers in Philanthropy Have Changed the Game", *www.genevaglobal.com.*

87 "Women and Giving" Rockefeller Philanthropy Advisors Philanthropy Roadmap.

88 Sellers, Patricia, "The Business of Being Oprah," *Fortune Magazine,* 1 April 2002.

89 Gillespie, E.M. (2019). *Women's Foundations and Funds: A Landscape Study.* Indianapolis, IN: Women's Philanthropy Institute, Indiana University Lilly School of Philanthropy.

90 www.womenmovingmillions.org.

91 Boris, Eileen and Annelise Orleck. "Feminism and the Labor Movement: A Century of Collaboration and Conflict". *New Labor Forum,* vol. 20, no.1, 2011, pp.33-41.

92 Boris, Eileen and Annelise Orleck. "Feminism and the Labor Movement: A Century of Collaboration and Conflict".

93 To learn more about Margaret Sanger see *www.plannedparenthood.com*; Blakemore, Erin, "The First Birth Control Pill Used Puerto Rican Women as Guinea Pigs", *www.history.com;* 11 March 2019, Little, Becky "Book talk Delivering "The Pill" Wasn't Easy", *National Geographic,* 18 December 2014; National Women's History Museum, "Margaret Sanger", *www.womenshistory.org.;,*Planned Parenthood, "Margaret Sanger- Our Founder". *Planned Parent Foundation of America,* June 2016; Sanger, Margaret, "Birth Control or Abortion?", *Birth Control Review,* Dec. 1918, 3-4, Margaret Sanger Microfilm, S70:809; Schmidt, Samantha, "Planned Parenthood to remove Margaret Sanger's name from N.Y. Clinic over views on eugenics", *The Washington Post,* 21 July 2020; Stewart, Nikita, "Planned Parenthood in N.Y. Disavows Margaret Sanger over Eugenics", *The New York Times,* 21 July 2020 and Wikipedia. "Margaret Sanger".

94 For more on Rachel Carson see Carson, Rachel, *The Edge of the Sea* Houghton Mifflin (1955), Mariner Books 1998; Carson, Rachel, *Silent Spring*, Houghton Mifflin 1962; Mariner Books 2002; Carson, Rachel, *The Sea Around Us*, Oxford University Press (1951), 1991; Carson, Rachel, *Under the Sea Wing*, (1941) Simon & Schuster, Penguin Group 1996; Lepore, Jill, "The Right Way to Remember Rachel Carson", *The New Yorker*, 19 March 2018; NRDC.org, "The Story of Silent Spring", 13 August 2015,"Rachel Carson, The Life and Legacy", *www.rachelcarson.org and lindalear.com* and Wikipedia, "Rachel Carson".

95 For more on Rosa Parks see New Frontier Theoharis, Jeanne, "How history got the Rosa Parks story wrong", *The Washington Post*, 1 December 2015 and Wikipedia, "Rosa Parks".

96 For more on Catherine Booth see CaringMagazine.org, "17 Things You Didn't Know About the Booth Family", Christian History Today, "Catherine Booth", *Chronicle.org*, "How William and Catherine Booth started The Salvation Army" and *Spartacus-educational.com*. "Catherine Booth".

97 For more on Katharine Drexel see *www.britannica.com*, "St. Katharine Drexel", Wikipedia, "Katharine Drexel" and *www.catholic.org*, "St. Katharine Drexel".

98 For more on Mary Baker Eddy see Wikipedia, "Mary Baker Eddy" and *www.christianscience.org*, "The Life of Mary Baker Eddy".

99 Kray, Laura J. et. al. "Feminine Charm: An Experimental Analysis of its Costs and Benefits in Negotiations", *Personality and Social Psychological Bulletin*, vol. 38, no. 10, 2012, pp 1343-1357.

100 Sciolino, Elaine, "Madeleine Albright's Audition", *The News York Times Magazine*, 22 September 1996.

101 Nayar, Vineet, "Women and Soft Power in Business", *Harvard Business Review*, 19 January 2011.

102 "New Research Shows Women are Better at Using Soft Skills Crucial for Effective Leadership and Superior Business Performance, Finds Korn Ferry Hay Group: Women Outperform Men in 11 of 12 Key Emotional Intelligence Competencies". Korn Ferry Hay Group 2016.

103 Weisberg, Yanna J. et. al. "Gender Differences in Personality across the Ten Aspects of the Big Five." *Front Psychol.* 2011; 2:178.

104 Picard, Caroline, "Prince Charles Called His Marriage to Diana a "Greek Tragedy" in Letters to Nancy Reagan, *Good Housekeeping Magazine*, 5 June 2017.

105 Pynchon, Victoria, "Opinion: Why it's ok to flirt your way to the top"., *cnn.com* 14 November 2012. 106 Betts, Hanna, "Why Flirting has always been woman's best weapon", *Telegraph*, 12 October 2012.

107 Harding, Eleanor, "Most Women 'flirt to get their way': Laying on the female charm can go a long way", *The Daily Mail*. 12 December 2012.

108 Kray, Laura J. et. al. "Feminine Charm: An Experimental Analysis of its Costs and Benefits in Negotiations", *Personality and Social Psychological Bulletin*, vol. 38, no. 10, 2012, pp 1343-1357.

109 Beard, Alison, "Mary Robinson" (Interview). *Harvard Business Review*, March 2013.

110 Cave, Damien, "Jacinda Ardern Sold a Drastic Lockdown With Straight Talk and Mom Jokes", *The New York Times*, 23 May 2020.

111 Spencer, Susan. *Briefcase Essentials: Discovering Your 12 Natural Talents for Achieving Success in Male-Dominated WorkPlaces*. Greenleaf Book Group (March 2011).

112 Rinehart, Keith, "Shakespeare's Cleopatra and England's Elizabeth", *Shakespeare Quarterly*, Volume 23, Issue 1, Winter 1972, Pages 81-86.

113 Kennedy, Caroline. *She Walks In Beauty: A Woman's Journey Through Poems*. Grand Central Publishing; Reprint Edition (March 15, 2016).

114 Koehn, Nancy, "Estee Lauder and the Market for Prestige Cosmetics", *Harvard Business School Case Study* No. 9-801-362, 27 February 2002.

115 Hurst, Fannie, "Glamour as Usual?" *New York Times Magazine* (March 29, 1942).

116 deNavarre, Maison G., "Are Further Restrictions Necessary for Cosmetics?" *Advertising & Selling* (February 1943), p. 153.

117 Tedlow, Richard S., "Charles Revson and Revlon", Harvard Business School working paper 00-032, Harvard Business School, Boston, MA 1999, p. 29.

118 Dove, "New Dove Report Research Finds Beauty Pressures Up, and Women and Girls Calling For Change", *Dove Self Esteem Project*, 21 June 2016.

119 Corkindale, Gill, "Exploiting Beauty in the Workplace", *Harvard Business Review*, 2 September 2011. See also Hakim, Catherine, *Erotic Capital: The Power of Attraction the Boardroom and the Bedroom*, Basic Books August 25, 2011.

120 Hatfield, Elaine. *Mirror Mirror: The Importance of Looks in Every Day Life*. SUNY Press. December 1, 1985.

121 Armstrong, Emily, "Pretty is a Set of Skills", *jezebel.com* 2 September 2013.

122 Banks, Ingrid. *Hair Matters; Beauty, Power and Black Women's Consciousness*. New York University Press. 2000.

123 Willie Morrow. *400 Years Without a Comb*, Black Publishers of San Diego (paperback) (1973).

124 Grier, William H. and Price M. Cobbs, *Black Rage*. Wipf and Stock (March 8, 2000).

125 Roberts, Blain. *Pageants, Parlors, and Pretty Women: Race and Beauty in the Twentieth-Century South*. The University of North Carolina Press. 2016.

126 Koehn, Nancy, Dwojeski, Anne E. Grundy, William, Helms, Eric and Katherine Miller, "Madam C.J. Walker: Entrepreneur, Leader and Philanthropist", *Harvard Business School Case Study* No. 9-807-145, 11 April 2011.

127 Riley, Sarah CE, and Christina Scharff. "Feminism versus Femininity? Exploring Feminist Dilemmas Through *Cooperative Inquiry Research", Feminism & Psychology*, vol. 23, no. 2, Mary 2013, pp 207-233.

128 Mohdin, Aamma "For Black Women Femininity and Feminism Are Not Mutually Exclusive", *Quartz*, 6 January 2018.

129 Mohdin, Aamma "For Black Women Femininity and Feminism Are Not Mutually Exclusive".

130 Mohndin, Aanna "For Black Women Femininity and Feminism Are Not Mutually Exclusive".

131 www.parlayhouse.com

132 Devereux-Mills, Andrea. *The Parlay Effect: How Female Connections Can Change The World.* Parlay House Books, January 7, 2020.

133 Zalis, Shelley, "Power of the Pack: Women Who Support Women Are More Successful", ForbesWoman, 6 March 2019.

134 "Collaboration's Hidden Tax on Women's Careers", *hbr.og*

135 Zalis, Shelley, Id.

136 Reardon, Dr. Kathleen Kelley, "Is Being Collaborative Really An Advantage For Women at Work" blog, *www.bigthinkedge.com.*

137 Cullinan, Renee. "In Collaborative Cultures, Women Carry More of the Weight", *Harvard Business Review*, 24 June 2018.

138 Tomlinson, Angie, "Celebrating the Collective Power of Women Supporting Women", *The West Australian,* 7 October 2018.

139 Woolf, Virginia, "A Room of One's Own", an extended essay first published in 1929 based on a series of lectures Woolf delivered at Newnhan College and Griton College, two womens colleges at Cambridge University in October 1928.

140 Lindbergh, Anne Morrow, *The Gift From The Sea.* Pantheon January 30, 1991 (reprint due to 50$^{th}$ anniversary).

141 Currey, Mason. *Daily Rituals: How Artists Work.* Knopf (April 23, 2013).

142 Schulte, Brigid. "A woman's greatest enemy? A lack of time to herself." *The Guardian,* 2019.

143 Schulte, Brigid. "A woman's greatest enemy? A lack of time to herself."

144 Forssen, Annika, S.K., and Gunilla Carlstedt. "It's Heavenly to be Alone!: A Room of One's Own as a Health-Promoting Resource for Women. Results from a Qualitative Study." *Scandinavian Journal of Public Health* 34, no. 2 (2006): 175-81.

145 Solly, Meilan. "RENAISSANCE NUN'S 'LAST SUPPER' PAINTING MAKES PUBLIC DEBUT AFTER 450 YEARS IN HIDING." *Smithsonian,* 21 Oct. 2019.

146 Solly, Meilan. "RENAISSANCE NUN'S 'LAST SUPPER' PAINTING MAKES PUBLIC DEBUT AFTER 450 YEARS IN HIDING."

147 For more on meditation and is importance see Bowlin, Stephanie L. "Relationships between mindfulness, self-control and psychological functioning." *Personality and Individual Differences* 52, no. 3 (2012); 411-415 and Friese, Malte et al. "Mindfulness meditation counteracts self-control depletion". *Consciousness and Cognition,* 21, no. 2 (2012): 1016-1022.

148 Wilson, Erica and Candice Harris. "Meaningful travel: Women, independent travel and the search for self and meaning." *Tourism* 54, no. 2 (2006): 161-172.

149 Milanie, Farzaneh, and Karla K. Morton. *Words Not Swords.* Syracuse University Press. 2011.

150 Florance, Charlotte. "Women's Empowerment Starts With Economic Freedom." *The Daily Signal,* 2014. Full Report: Miller, Terry. "Economic Freedom: Revolutionary Empowerment for Women." *The Heritage Foundation,* 2008.

151 Samson, Kurt. "Stronger Social Support Shown to Improve Early Breast Cancer Outcomes", *Oncology Times*: October 10th, 2011. Volume 33. Issue 19. Pp. 36-38.

152 Id.

153 Uzzi, Brian. "Research: Men and Women Need Different Kinds of Networks to Succeed.", *Harvard Business Review,* 2019.

154 Cronin, Anne M. "Domestic Friends: Women's Friendships, Motherhood and Inclusive Intimacy." *The Sociological Review* 63, no. 3 (August 2015); 662-79.

155 Bateson, Mary Catherine. *Composing a Life,* Knopf. May 10, 2001.

156 Michelson, Joan. "Women's Choices: A Model "Redsign of Life". *Forbes,* 2019.

157 158 www.longevity.stanford.edu.

159 See *www.barbara-huson.com. Prince Charming Isn't Coming: How Women Get Smart About Money*. Penguin Books, Revised Edition (April 24, 2007)

160 Pfeffer, Jeffrey, "Women and the Uneasy Embrace of Power", *Harvard Business Review,* 4 August 2010.

161 Rikleen, Lauren Stiller, "Power Play Strategies for Women", *Harvard Business Review*, 2 July 2012.

162 Flynn, Jill, Kathryn Heath and Mary Davis Holt, "Three Ways Women Can Make Office Politics Work For Them", *Harvard Business Review,* 8 March 2012.

163 Flynn, Jill, Kathryn Heath and Mary Davis Holt, "Three Ways Women Can Make Office Politics Work For Them",

164 Arpin, Sarah N., Monica Y. Bartlett, and Piercarlo Valdesolo. "The paradox of power: The relationship between self-esteem and gratitude." *The Journal of Social Psychology* 160, no 1 (April 2019): 27-38.

165 O'Reilly, Julie D. *Bewitched Again: Supernaturally Powerful Women on Televisoin, 1996-2011.* McFarland, 2013.

166 Fels, Dr. Anne, "Do Women Lack Ambition?", *Harvard Business Review.* 2004.

167 Sheryl Sandberg's Commencement Speech to Barnard College Class of 2011. (www.youtube.com)

168 Slaughter, Anne Marie, *"Why Women Still Can't Have It All"*, The Atlantic, July/August 2012.

169 Venker, Suzanne, "Should it be illegal to be a stay-at-home mom? Why feminists are so frustrated." *Fox News.* 2017.

170 Berg, Maxine, "Women's Work and the Industrial Revolution". *Refresh* 12 (Spring 1991).

171 'Employment of Women in War Production." *Social Security Bulletin*, 1942.

172 Berg, Maxine. "Women's Work and the Industrial Revolution".

173 Sonderson, Shobba, in "Work-life balance-implications for working women," (International Conference on Sustainable Development, 2014).

174 Sonderson, Shobba, in "Work-life balance-implications for working women."

175 Ely, Robin J. 2020. "What's Really Holding Women Back?" *Harvard Business Review,* March – April Issue, 2020

176 Petriglieri, Jennifer, "How Dual Career Couples Can Work Through The Coronovirus Crisis", *Harvard Business Review.* 27 March 2020.

177 Claman, Priscilla, "Working Parents, Your Family Needs a Board of Directors", *Harvard Business Review*, 8 July 2020.

178 Plett, Heather, "What if we were unafraid of our own power?" *www.heatherplett.com* May 2014.

179 Fabrega, Lisa. "The Confidence Experiment: Why Women Leaders Fear Being Powerful & What We Can Do About It". *www.lisafabgrega.com*.

180 Yonika, Maya. "Why Women Are Afraid Of Their Own Power"., *www.medium.com*, 19 June 2019.

181 Hymovitz, Kay, "Review of Woman's Inhumanity to Woman: by Phyllis Chesler", *Commentary Magazine* May 2002.

182 Chesler, Phyllis, *Woman's Inhumanity to Woman*. Lawrence Hill Books, 2009. See also Tannen, Deborah, Review of Woman's Inhumanity to Woman, *The Washington Post,* 10 March 2002 and Greenspan, Miriam, "When Women Injure Women: Woman's Inhumanity to Woman"., *Tikkun,* Vol. 17., Issue 3. May/June 2002.

183 Chesler, Phyllis, "Some Women are Inhumane to Other Women", *www.psychreg.org* 3 December 2018.

184 Brock, Barbara L. "When Sisterly Support Changes to Sabotage". *Journal of Women in Educational Leadership*, vol. 6, no. 3, July 2008, pp. 211-226.

185 Cooper, Marianne. "Why Women (Sometimes) Don't Help Other Women." *The Atlantic,* 30 July 2016.

186 Marcus, Bonnie, "The Dark Side of Female Rivalry in the Workplace and What to Do About It"., *Forbes Magazine,* 13 January 2016.

187 McNulty, Anne Welsh "Don't Underestimate the Power of Women Supporting Each Other at Work" *Harvard Business Review.*

188 Hewlett, Sylvia Ann. *Executive Presence: The Missing Link Between Merit and Success*. Harper Business, June 3, 2014.

189 Farrow, Ronan, *Catch and Kill: Lies, Spies and a Conspiracy To Protect Predators*. Little Brown and Company. (October 15, 2019).

190Kantor, Jodi and Meghan Twohey. *"She Said: Breaking The Sexual Harassment Story That Helped Ignite a Movement"*. Penguin Press (September, 10, 2019).

191 Bower, Tim. "The #MeToo Backlash", *Harvard Business Review*, 27 August 2019.

192 Bower, Tim. "The #MeToo Backlash".

193 Monllos, Kristina. "Inside Agencies: Men and Women Still Struggle to Deal with the Fall out of #MeToo". *Digiday*, 2 January 2020.

194 Monllos, Kristina. "Inside Agencies: Men and Women Still Struggle to Deal with the Fall out of #MeToo".

195 Elsesser, Kim. "The Latest Consequence of #MeToo: Not Hiring Women", *Forbes Magazine*. 6 September 2019.

196 Pauly, Madison. "She Said. He Sued. How Libel Law is Being Turned Against Me Too Accusers", *Mother Jones*, 15 February 2020.

197 North, Anna. "7 Positive Changes That Have Come from the #MeToo Movement." *Vox*, 4 October 2019.

# Acknowledgements

My husband Robert E. Carr

Jessica Bacal

Nan-b de Gaspe Beaubien

Linda Cashdan

Donna Cohen

Allyson Einbinder

Abigail Elwell

James Grubman, Ph.D.

David Howell

Ashley Kaitz

John M. Hughes

Jody Snider

# About the Author

**Patricia M. Annino** has been named as one of the Best Lawyers in America and a Top 50 Female Massachusetts SuperLawyer. She is the author of four books, “Women & Money: A Practical Guide to Estate Planning”, “Women in Family Business: What Keeps You Up at Night?”, “Cracking the $$ Code: What Successful Men Know (and you don’t yet)” and “It’s More than Money: Protect Your Legacy”, all available at *www.amazon.com*.

Women & Money LLC

Made in the USA
Coppell, TX
13 March 2021

51688435R00108